12/09/06

D03383081

Modern Library Chronicles

CHINUA ACHEBE on Africa

KAREN ARMSTRONG on Islam

DAVID BERLINSKI on mathematics

RICHARD BESSEL on Nazi
Germany

ALAN BRINKLEY on the Great
Depression

IAN BURUMA on modern Japan

IAN BURUMA AND AVISHAI
MARGALIT on Occidentalism

JAMES DAVIDSON on the Golden
Age of Athens

SEAMUS DEANE on the Irish

LAWRENCE M. FRIEDMAN on
law in America

PAUL FUSSELL on World War II
in Europe

MARTIN GILBERT on the Long
War, 1914–1945

PETER GREEN on the Hellenistic
Age

JAN T. GROSS on the fall of
Communism

ALISTAIR HORNE on the age of
Napoleon

PAUL JOHNSON on the
Renaissance

TONY JUDT on the Cold War

FRANK KERMODE on the age of
Shakespeare

JOEL KOTKIN on the city

HANS KÜNG on the Catholic
Church

BERNARD LEWIS on the Holy
Land

FREDRIK LOGEVALL on the
Vietnam War

MARK MAZOWER on the
Balkans

JOHN MICKLETHWAIT AND
ADRIAN WOOLDRIDGE on
the company

PANKAJ MISHRA on the rise of
modern India

ANTHONY PAGDEN on peoples
and empires

RICHARD PIPES on Communism

COLIN RENFREW on prehistory

JOHN RUSSELL on the museum

KEVIN STARR on California

ALEXANDER STILLE on fascist
Italy

CATHARINE R. STIMPSON on the
university

NORMAN STONE on World War I

MICHAEL STÜRMER on the
German Empire

STEVEN WEINBERG on science

BERNARD WILLIAMS on
freedom

A. N. WILSON on London

ROBERT S. WISTRICH on the
Holocaust

GORDON S. WOOD on the
American Revolution

JAMES WOOD on the novel

THE

AMERICAS

FELIPE FERNÁNDEZ-ARMESTO

THE
AMERICAS

A Hemispheric History

A MODERN LIBRARY CHRONICLES BOOK

THE MODERN LIBRARY

NEW YORK

2003 Modern Library Edition

Copyright © 2003 by Felipe Fernández-Armesto

All rights reserved under International and Pan-American Copyright
Conventions. Published in the United States by Modern Library,
an imprint of The Random House Ballantine Publishing Group,
a division of Random House, Inc., New York, and simultaneously
in Canada by Random House of Canada Limited, Toronto.

MODERN LIBRARY and the TORCHBEARER Design are registered
trademarks of Random House, Inc.

LIBRARY OF CONGRESS CATALOGING-IN-PUBLICATION DATA
Fernández-Armesto, Felipe.
The Americas: a hemispheric history / Felipe Fernández-Armesto.
p.   cm.—(A Modern Library chronicles book; 13)
Includes bibliographical references (p.   ) and index.
ISBN 0-375-50476-1
1. America—History. I. Title. II. Modern Library chronicles; 13.
E18 .F39   2003
909'.09812—dc21 2002040779

Modern Library website address: www. modernlibrary.com

Printed in the United States of America on acid-free paper

CONTENTS

LIST OF MAPS   ix

1. AMERICAS? AMERICA?   3

2. BETWEEN COLONIZATIONS:
   THE AMERICAS' FIRST "NORMALCY"   21

3. COLONIAL AMERICAS: DIVERGENCE AND ITS LIMITS   55

4. THE INDEPENDENCE ERA   99

5. INDEPENDENCE: THE NEW DEPENDENCY   129

6. THE AMERICAN CENTURY   159

7. RETROSPECT AND PROSPECTS: GRINGOS
   AND GO-GETTERS   189

BIBLIOGRAPHICAL ESSAY   207

INDEX   225

LIST OF MAPS

THE DIVERSITY OF CENTRAL AND SOUTH AMERICA   xi

THE COLONIALS, C. 1650   xii

THE AMERICAS, 1830   xiii

THE AMERICAS   xiv

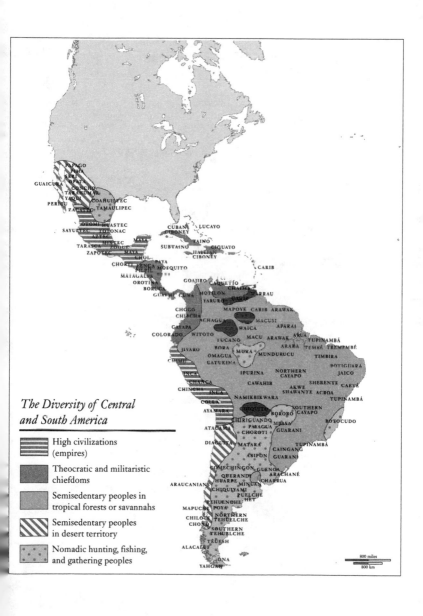

The Diversity of Central and South America

- High civilizations (empires)
- Theocratic and militaristic chiefdoms
- Semisedentary peoples in tropical forests or savannahs
- Semisedentary peoples in desert territory
- Nomadic hunting, fishing, and gathering peoples

800 miles
800 km

PAPAGO
PIMA
SERI
OPATA
GUAICURA CONCHO
TARAHUMARA
YAQUI
PERICU COAHUILTEC
ZACATEC TAMAULIPEC

OTOMI HUASTEC
SAYULTEC TOTONAC
TARASCA MIXTEC MAYA
ZAPOTEC MAYA
CHOL
CHORTI LENCA MOSQUITO
MATAGALPA SUBU
OROTINA PAYA
BORUCA
GUAYMI CUNA

CUBANY LUCAYO
CIBONEY
TAINO
SUBTAINO CIGUAYO
HAITIAN
CIBONEY
CARIB

GOAJIRO CAIMETTO
MOTILON CHAIMA GUARRAU
YARURO TARIO

CHOCO MAPOYE CARIB ARAWAK
CHIBCHA ACHAGUA MACUSI
CAYAPA WAICA APARAI
COLORADO WITOTO ARAWAK ARUA
JIVARO FUCANO MACU TUPINAMBÁ
BORA OMAGUA ARABA TEMNÉ TREMEMBÉ
CHIMU GATUKINA MUKA MUNDURUCU TIMBIRA
IPURINA NORTHERN POTIGUARA
INCA CAYAPO JAICO
CHANCA CAWAHIB SHERENTE CAETÉ
CHINCHA AKWE CAETÉ
INCA NAMIKBIKWARA SHAWANTE ACROA
COLLA CHIQUITO TUPINAMBÁ
AYAMARA SOUTHERN
CHIRIGUANO BORORO CAYAPO
ATACAMA PAYAGUA MBAYA BOTOCUDO
DIAGUITA MATARA CHOROTI GUARANI
ABIPON CAINGANG
COMECHINGON GUENOA TUPINAMBÁ
QUERANDI GUARANI
ARAUCANIANS HUARPE MINUAN ARACHANÉ
CHIQUIYAMI PUELCHE CHARRUA
MAPUCHE PEHUENCHE HET
POYA
CHILOTE NORTHERN
CHONO TEHUELCHE
SOUTHERN
TEHUELCHE
ALACALUF TEUESH
ONA
YAHGAN

ATLANTIC OCEAN

Transatlantic fleet to Seville

Gulf of Mexico

AUDENCIA OF
NUEVO GALICIA
(1549)

Monterrey
Durango Saltillo
Zacatecas
San Luis Potosí

Transatlantic fleet
to Havana

VICEROYALTY OF
NEW SPAIN

Guadalajara

Guanajuato
Valladolid

AUDENCIA OF
MEXICO
(1529)

Mexico
City

Veracruz

Havana

AUDENCIA OF
SANTO DOMINGO
(1511)

Santiago

Santo
Domingo

San Juan

Transatlantic fleet from Seville

Oaxaca
Acapulco

Campeche
Belize
(Br.)

Guatemala
Antigua

AUDENCIA OF
GUATEMALA
(1544)

Granada

Mérida

Caribbean Sea

Transpacific fleet from Manila

Panama

Coro
Caracas

Cumaná

Maracaibo
Mérida

Stabrok
(Dutch.)

AUDENCIA OF
SANTA FE
(1548)

Orinoco

Paramaribo (Dutch)

Surinam
(Br. 1650)

Cayenne (Fr.)

Transpacific fleet to Manila

PACIFIC OCEAN

Galapagos
Islands

Quito

PRESIDENCIA
OF QUITO
(1563)

Santa Fe
de Bogotá

Belém de Pará (Port.)

Maranhão (Port.)

Ceará (Port.)

VICEROYALTY
OF PERU

Lima

AUDENCIA
OF LIMA
(1543)

Dutch Brazil (1630)

Recife

La Paz

Bahia

La Plata

PRESIDENCIA
OF CHARCAS
(1559)

Asunción

Portuguese Capidancies

The Colonials, c. 1650

———— Viceroyalty boundaries
○ Audencia capitals
- - - - - Audencia boundaries
——— Other colonial boundaries
• Major provincial cities
○ Mining towns
⟶ Trade routes

CAPTAINCY-
GENERALCY
OF CHILE
(1606)

Santiago

São Paulo

Rio de Janeiro

Buenos Aires

Falkland
Islands

800 miles
800 km

Greenland
(Denmark)

BRITISH NORTH AMERICA

[disputed]

UNITED STATES

ATLANTIC OCEAN

MEXICO
(1821)

Gulf of Mexico

Mexico • • Veracruz

Cuba
(Spain)

Lucayas /
Bahama Islands
(Britain)

Puerto Rico
(Spain)

BRITISH
HONDURAS

Jamaica
(Britain)

HAITI
(1804)

Windward Islands
(French, British, Danish
and Dutch possessions)

UNITED PROVINCES
OF CENTRAL AMERICA
(1821)
[dissolved by 1839]

Caribbean Sea

Caracas • • Trinidad (Britain)

VENEZUELA
(1830)

BRITISH GUIANA
DUTCH GUIANA
FRENCH GUIANA

GRAN COLOMBIA
(1819)
[dissolved
by 1830]

Bogotá •

COLOMBIA
(1831)

Galapagos
Islands

Quito •

ECUADOR
(1830)

PERU
(1821)

Lima •

BRAZIL
(1822)

• Salvador

• La Paz

BOLIVIA
(1825)

PACIFIC OCEAN

PARAGUAY
(1811)

São Paulo •

• Asunción

• Rio de Janeiro

CHILE
(1817)

Buenos Aires 🏵🏵 URUGUAY (1828)
          • Montevideo

UNITED PROVINCES
RIO DE LA PLATA (1816)

ARGENTINE
CONFEDERATION (1825)

PATAGONIA

The Americas, 1830

■ Colonies and other dependent areas

Falkland
Islands

800 miles

800 km

CANADA

UNITED STATES

ATLANTIC OCEAN

Greenland

Gulf of Mexico

Mexico City ⊙ MEXICO

Havana
CUBA
BAHAMAS
Port-au-Prince
JAMAICA
Kingston
HAITI
PUERTO RICO
Santo Domingo
DOMINICAN REPUBLIC

ST. KITTS & NEVIS (Basseterre)
ANTIGUA & BARBUDA (St. John's)
DOMINICA (Roseau)
ST. LUCIA (Castries)

Belize City
BELIZE
HONDURAS
Tegucigalpa
Guatemala City
GUATEMALA
San Salvador
EL SALVADOR
Managua
NICARAGUA
San José
COSTA RICA
PANAMA
Panama City

Caribbean Sea

BARBADOS (Bridgetown)
ST. VINCENT (Kingstown)
GRENADA (St. George's)
TRINIDAD & TOBAGO (Port of Spain)

Caracas ⊙ VENEZUELA
GUYANA
Georgetown ⊙
Paramaribo
SURINAME
FRENCH GUIANA

Bogotá ⊙ COLOMBIA

Quito ⊙ ECUADOR

GALAPAGOS ISLANDS (Ecuador)

PERU

BRAZIL

Lima ⊙

La Paz ⊙ BOLIVIA
Sucre
Brasília ⊙

PACIFIC OCEAN

PARAGUAY
Asunción ⊙

CHILE

Santiago ⊙

Buenos Aires ⊙ ⊙ URUGUAY
Montevideo

ARGENTINA

FALKLAND ISLANDS (Great Britain)

The Americas

■ Colonies and other dependent areas

⊙ Capital cities
(independent countries only;
Windward Islands capitals
shown in parentheses)

800 miles
800 km

THE

AMERICAS

AMERICAS? AMERICA?

Americans bicker over the name of Americans. To the chorus in *West Side Story*, America is a foreign land, where some of them "like to be," a sentiment apparently inaccessible to them in Puerto Rico. Canadians write to newspapers in the United States complaining that the citizens of one country have usurped the appellation of Americans. The Spanish intellectual Américo Castro was so called because he was born on a boat on the way to Argentina. In much of South America the people of the United States are called *norteamericanos*, whereas the northernmost Americans are actually Inuit and the United States reaches only the forty-eighth parallel. A character in *Barcelona*, Whit Stillman's film about U.S. expatriates trying to cope with anti-Americanism, resents the Spanish term *estadounidense* because it makes him feel despised as "dense." Many of the names by which Americans call one another—Anglos, Afros, *indios*, Latinos, Caucasians—tug at other continents. The privileged names now enjoyed by some minorities—Native Americans, *indígenas*, First Nations—imply an imperfect sense of belonging in everyone else. No usage suits everybody.

Yet America was once "the New World"—pure and simple. It was possible to imagine it as a single category, a single polity, the home of a huge, embracing identity. Pan-Americanism no longer exists, except as piety or rhetoric. Like "Europe," America is a Humpty-Dumpty continent. It has to be painfully reconstructed after the ravages of nationalism, across the fissures and fractures between which rival identities have formed. This book is an attempt at mental reconstruction of the hemisphere; an effort to see it whole and to trace a common history that embraces all the Americas.

AMERICAN SINGULARITY

How many Americas are there? Once, at least in the eyes of beholders who looked at the hemisphere from outside, there was only one. America possessed unity and integrity of a sort, long before it was well delineated. The term entered our languages in the singular. Amerigo Vespucci (or, at least, a writer using his byline) reported the first lands known as "America" from the coasts of what are now Venezuela, Guiana, and Brazil. Martin Waldseemüller, the cosmographer who coined the name in Amerigo's honor on a map and an accompanying treatise in 1507, rapidly regretted it; he realized that the honor of the discoveries he had attributed to Vespucci really belonged to Columbus. In his next map he suppressed the name, but it was too late. "America" extended, in contemporary imaginations, over the whole of an ill-defined hemisphere, which seemed to grow as successive expeditions explored further, unsuspected parts of it. The unity of the New World was apparent to most early explorers who reconnoitered it and early European cartographers who drew it. Some of them, at first, split it into two with a very narrow strait; others showed the New World as what we think of today as South America, while representing North America as a promontory of Asia. But the convention of showing the whole hemisphere as a single large landmass was well established in the second decade of the sixteenth century.

This is an odder, more intriguing fact than it may at first seem, since it was easier, in the years when the idea of

America was first introduced to European minds, to deny the hemisphere altogether—dismissing the claim that it existed as fraud or delusion—or to classify it as part of Asia. European geographers in antiquity and the Middle Ages speculated about the existence of an unexplored land-mass in the unfrequented recesses of the western ocean. But belief in it was a minority indulgence, derided by skeptics. The idea that something as big and discrete as a "new world" lurked unseen, waiting to be discovered, seemed implausible to the Old World. Even writers of the medieval equivalent of science fiction—romances of seaborne chivalry—generally preferred to speckle the Atlantic with islands as settings for their heroes' adventures. So did the makers of speculative sea charts (though a series survives of fifteenth-century maps that also depict a western continent, named after the daughters of Hesperus from the legend of Hercules, who raided their garden for golden apples).

Most cosmographers reviewing projects for ocean cross-ings in the fifteenth century dismissed the possibility that exploration would uncover a new continent. They thought they knew all the world there was. Even Columbus, who found a route to America, was disinclined to believe that such a place existed. Though his geographical notions were mercurial, and he was inclined to change his mind accord-ing to the fancies and prejudices of his audience, he gen-erally favored the view that the world was too small to accommodate an unknown hemisphere; the "new world" he claimed to have discovered was, in his own estimation, really just a new part of the old one—the easternmost extremities of Eurasia, the "Indies" that the ancients had labored to reach.

Nevertheless, in the century or so preceding Columbus's voyages, the idea that something like America might really exist did gain some ground. Partly this was because of the movement we loosely call the Renaissance—the progressive rediscovery in western Europe of texts from classical antiquity. Mainstream geographical tradition in antiquity knew roughly how big the world was. In the third century B.C. the librarian Eratosthenes had measured it with tolerable accuracy. He proposed a value of about twenty-five thousand miles at the equator, in modern terms, using a mixture of trigonometry, which was infallible, and measurement, which was open to quibble. But there was clearly room for "another world"—"the Antipodes," as it was called by geographers who believed in it.

A number of fifteenth-century "humanists"—pursuers, that is, of the anthropocentric curriculum recommended by classical scholarship—drew attention to ancient speculations about the Antipodes. In 1423 one of the most suggestive ancient geographical texts arrived in Latin Christendom: Strabo's defense, written in Greek in the first century B.C. of a picture of the world traditional since the time of Homer. Strabo placed the supposed unknown continent roughly where Columbus or one of the other Atlantic navigators of the time might have hoped to find it. "It may be," he wrote, "that in this same temperate zone there are actually two inhabited worlds, or even more, and in particular in the proximity of the parallel through Athens that is drawn across the Atlantic." In the context of Strabo's thought as a whole it seems that this observation was intended ironically; but irony is notoriously difficult to detect in texts from an unfamiliar time or culture, and some of Columbus's contemporaries took the passage literally. As soon as Columbus returned from his first Atlantic crossing, humanist geographers began to speculate that he had reached the Antipodes. The more people learned about it, the more the identification solidified. The parts of the American mainland and islands—despite their vastness and their multitudinous diversity—fused into one.

Yet, from another point of view, it was a mistake to think of America as one. People who lived there before Columbus arrived had no such notion—they knew it too well. The unity of the hemisphere was imposed by imaginations that could barely suspect how enormous it was, or by minds anxious to shrink it to manageable proportions, so that it could be easily skirted by merchants bound for Oriental spiceries. Old World minds seemed to resist the truth about American size and complexity. It took a long time for the reality of America to sink in. In the mid-1520s, Verrazano thought he could see the Pacific from the Atlantic off the Carolina coast. Most sixteenth-century maps squeezed North America into narrow proportions. English colonists in Virginia in the early seventeenth century thought they would be able to reach the "South Sea" by overland march. The early navigators of the Mississippi expected the great river to flow into a sea that washed China.

As knowledge of the scale and variety of the Americas gradually grew and began to shadow reality, minds did not adjust by abandoning unified conceptions; America remained one big place. Creole patriots in the American regions of the Spanish monarchy called themselves "Americans" long before the term became current in what is now the United States. In symbolic seventeenth- and eighteenth-century depictions of the continents, there is always only one America. The eighteenth-century "dispute of the New World"—a long-running debate among intellectuals about how to classify America and its products—was conducted largely in terms of hemisphere-wide generalizations. European commentators criticized America as a whole; when Georges-Louis Buffon (1707–1788) and Cornelius De Pauw (1734–1799) derided America as a degenerate and degenerating place, which produced only stunted species, inferior people—effete men, insensitive women—and regressive civilizations, they attributed these unsettling qualities to the entire hemisphere. For De Pauw in his *Recherches philosophiques sur les Américains,* Patagonian giants were as implausible as philosophical Hurons, or albinos in Darién, or Amazons along the Amazon; they were all delusions of the kind that made the hemisphere seem wonderful, when really, he claimed, it was woeful. He generalized about the climate: it was cold and wet, damp and putrid everywhere. This was only slightly more unhelpful than the equal and opposite generalizations advocated by apologists for America, such as Antoine-Joseph Pernéty (1716–1801), who insisted that the climate was everywhere benign.

So, like it or loathe it, people still thought of the hemisphere as one. The Founding Fathers of the United States imagined a political union that might ultimately embrace the entire New World, with their own republic as "the nest," in Jefferson's phrase, of "all America, North and South." (In a sense, their successors maintained this tradition; the Monroe Doctrine also treated the Americas as a single, privileged arena where only American intervention or hegemony was welcome. A feeble version of the same doctrine today represents the Americas outside the Union as Uncle Sam's "backyard.") Even some of the indigenous peoples gradually came to share the unitary vision imposed by outsiders' eyes and to develop a sense of solidarity, which now embraces others who, to their ancestors, were enemies or unknown. Mapuche and Micmac, Yupik and Yamaná are all today "Native Americans." Some of them even speak of sharing "Turtle Island."

THE MULTIPLICATION OF AMERICAS

Yet in other respects history has shivered the unitary vision into fragments. Political boundaries carve the continent, as if with a hacksaw in the north, where most of the dividing lines are ruled straight across the map, and a jigsaw in the south, where political frontiers lurch across complex topography. No part of the Americas has ever been a completely effective melting pot, and everywhere there are unassimilated lumps of multiple Americas. There are still, happily, innumerable indigenous Americas, inhabited by peoples who never lost their precolonial identities or who have developed or recovered them during or after colonial times. The Mani map, a Yucatec depiction of the world from the early colonial period, shows the local community's lands in great detail, with the rest of the world relegated to the edges; this is typically ethnocentric and expresses a widely exemplified, robust sense of community that seems to survive every stress.

Moreover, there are threads and patches of cultural distinctiveness woven by immigrant communities all over the hemisphere. In Brazil you can be German or Japanese without ceasing to be Brazilian. Some Patagonians worship in Welsh without compromising their allegiance to Argentina. New Yorkers who lobby for Israel or Bostonians who subscribe to Noraid are not engaged in un-American activities. The United States is partly, importantly, composed of hyphenated identities; Americans there are no less American for being Italian-American or Irish-American or Polish-American, or, as they say in the English of America, "whatever." In Buenos Aires I had a taxi driver who spoke nothing but my own family's ancestral language, Galician. He explained to me that there were so many of our fellow countrymen in B.A. that it was unnecessary to be able to speak anything else. Galician-American takes its place alongside all the others. How can one generalize across so much cultural complexity?

It is hardly necessary to stress the hemisphere's political disunity; the successor states of the Spanish monarchy in America multiplied along the fissures of the colonial political system. Although, so far, the three giant states, Brazil, Canada, and the United States, have survived attempts to break them up, the process is not altogether over; in Canada secession has been a livelier issue in our time than ever before. There are probably more secessionists— certainly more enthusiasts for "states' rights"—in parts of the United States today than at any time since the Civil War. I have been amazed, traveling in the United States, at how state boundaries that look like arbitrary pencil strokes, easily erasable, often enclose a fierce and heartfelt sense of belonging. The extreme case is that of Texas, where an independent republic once flourished, where the Lone Star flag waves everywhere as a memento of uniqueness, and where—alone among the states of the Union—you can see people in what amounts to the state dress: Stetson and cowboy boots. No other state has quite so pronounced a protonational culture, but you can see the beginnings of something similar growing up almost everywhere, as states' histories get longer and whatever is distinctive becomes more prized. The Caribbean federations set up by retreating empires in modern times have crumbled. Mexico, the Americas' most fissile state in the nineteenth century, which lost most of its territory to rebellion and war, still seems imperfectly amalgamated; in Yucatán I once watched a beauty contest in which the attractions of the Yucatec girls seemed to arouse in the audience more chauvinism than concupiscence, more illusions of separatism than of sex.

Americas multiply in memories and fancies. There are lost Americas and imaginary Americas. Innumerable eutopias and utopias have been found or fancied in America. Most of them have been responses—variously adventurous and eccentric—to the opportunity of human re-creation represented by a "New World." In Fourier's Harmony, which his followers tried to build in America, orgies were organized with a degree of bureaucratic particularity that seemed certain to kill passion. In America, as John Adolphus Etzler proposed to remodel it in 1833, mountains were to be flattened and forests "ground to dust" to make building cement; in practice, this is not all that different from the way things have turned out in parts of the United States. In Étienne Cabet's Icaria—the blueprint for several socialist experiments in community building in the early United States—clothes were to be made of elastic to make the principle of equality "suit people of different sizes." Brigham Young imagined a paradise of latter-day saints on the shores of Salt Lake. Disneyland and its imitators are the latest and least of a long tradition of American fairylands.

Persisting beside them are legendary Americas, which have survived in tribal memory since the first father sprang from the land; these coexist uneasily with archaeologists' America, peopled from Asia during the Ice Age and therefore united at a level invisible in culture and undetectable in stratigraphy. When Hugh Brody sat on Canada's Royal Commission on Aboriginal Peoples, his workshop got "stuck in an intellectual quagmire" when a Cree Ph.D. student argued that archaeologists were ignorant and that native origin-myths were unarguably consistent; almost everywhere the ancestors had emerged from prehuman origins in the places their descendants occupied. They did not have to cross Ice Age Beringia to reach America. They just belonged. Everyone has his own private America. For John Donne, his mistress was his America; for Pablo Neruda, his America was his mistress.

"America" is a term even elastic enough to extend beyond America, as ordinarily understood, into or across the Atlantic and Pacific. Most people would admit as part of the Americas all the Caribbean islands, Fernando de Noronha, and probably the Falklands or Malvinas on the Atlantic side, and in the Pacific, archipelagoes such as the Revillagigedo and Galápagos Islands, which at present form part of the sovereign territory of American states. But in the Atlantic, what about Greenland and Bermuda? And if they are admitted as American, why not islands farther out in the ocean? Some people think of Ireland as "essentially an American country" that happens to lie on the wrong side of the Atlantic; this is not as daft as it seems at first, since Ireland shares some American historical experiences of British imperialism. Angola could justifiably feature in a history of the Americas in the eighteenth and nineteenth centuries, when it was virtually an offshore dependency of Brazil, linked by winds, chained by the slave trade. In the Pacific, by the same reasoning, the Philippines might count as American. Under Spanish rule, they belonged administratively and culturally to a unit that included most of the Americas; they were populated by people the Spaniards called *indios*, using the same general name as was applied to the indigenous peoples of the New World.

From 1898 until 1946 the archipelago was the remotest territory of the United States. Today aspects of Filipino culture—folksy, politicized Catholicism, Hispanic architecture, creole-like foods, and a style of democracy that is vibrant and violent, dynamic and fragile—all remind the visitor of much of Latin America. Less equivocal, perhaps, are the cases of Hawaii, the Aleutian Islands, and Guam; these are all American in the sense of belonging to the United States. Is there any better-than-arbitrary reason for excluding them from America? Then there are Britons who want to secede from the European Union and join NAFTA. The more inclusive we make the name of America, the frailer its unity becomes; the valid generalizations diminish, the anomalies multiply.

THE EXCEPTIONALIST TEMPTATION

In our history books—even in works that help to make us aware of the plurality and diversity of the hemisphere—there are usually only two Americas. On the one hand appear the United States and Canada, which, in effect, means the United States alone, with Canada tacked on for marginal consideration. On the other hand lies all the rest of the hemisphere (and whatever else one may wish to include). This categorization is so familiar that it passes unquestioned outside problem-fraught specialist literature. Yet it is puzzling. It is monstrously unbalanced. The population of the United States and Canada together amounts to nearly 300 million people. The rest of the hemisphere, even if we omit the doubtful outliers, contains more than half as many again. The habit of drawing a line roughly at the Rio Grande does not correspond with any objective method of categorization; the United States and Canada possess together no obvious geographical unity. Geographers usually include Mexico in North America, but when we use the term "North America" in an attempt to capture some sense of cultural unity, we usually, implicitly, leave Mexico out. Yet Mexico also forms a trio with Canada and the States in NAFTA—a grouping that reflects the economic realities of North American interdependence. A common assumption is that the hemisphere divides culturally into Anglo-American and Latin American moieties; if so, the conventional categorization does not reflect any such divide.

Belize, Guiana, the Malvinas, and much of the Caribbean belong culturally to Anglo-America: English-speaking, with an English institutional inheritance. Indeed, like most of Canada, those parts of the Americas are more "Anglo" than the United States, since they shared in British imperialism for longer and remain in the Commonwealth or the British state. Some of them even maintain an "Anglo" tradition that seems alien in Canada and the States; they play soccer and cricket—the culture bestowed or inflicted on the world by England's "public schools." Just as Anglo-America overspills Canada and the States, so Latin America seeps inside them. Culturally, much of the U.S. Southwest and Florida belongs to Latin America, as does the U.S. territory of Puerto Rico. If French Guiana and the French Caribbean belong to Latin America, so, logically, must Québec. Saint Barthélemy, the Netherlands Antilles, and Surinam were colonized from Sweden and Holland, yet contiguity sucks them into Latin America. Saint Thomas and the Virgin Islands were both Danish colonies; yet the former tends to be classed inside Latin America, the latter outside it.

U.S. exceptionalism—a doctrine often evoked to justify a two-headed classification of the Americas—is illogical.

All peoples think of themselves as exceptional—ironically, it is one of the things they all have in common. Exceptionalism is universal and therefore self-subverting. Genuine historic communities always differ from their neighbors in some ways; one might as well treat Nicaraguan exceptionalism or Paraguayan exceptionalism as a reason for separating the history of those countries from that of the rest of the New World. But when exceptional cases are examined in detail the similarities usually outweigh the differences. The differences cannot be appreciated unless in comparative perspective; the exceptionalist hypothesis always has to be tested by contemplating what is said to be exceptional alongside what is supposed to be normative. Americans' trouble is not exceptionalism—they are all too much like the rest of us. Many of the supposedly good things about U.S. exceptionalism, such as the dynamic wealth creation, the democracy, the accessibility of opportunity, the cult of civil liberty, the tradition of tolerance, and the supposedly bad things, such as the trash capitalism, the excessive privileges of wealth, the selective illiberalism, the dumbed-down popular culture, the stagnancy of politics, the tetchiness and ignorance that veil the States from the world—all these are common virtues and evils of many modern societies, throughout and indeed beyond the Americas. Only the intensity with which they are concentrated in the United States makes the States exceptional and, therefore, in another sense, representative. Even the most resolute believers in U.S. exceptionalism now tend to see it as a "double-edged sword"—partly a source of weakness, which makes the United States exceptional chiefly in evincing more extreme forms of other people's commonplace vices, such as myopic patriotism, morbid religiosity, and conflictive insistence on one's rights.

In any case, if the United States were genuinely exceptional, the category in which it belongs could not properly include Canada, whereas the criteria that justify the exclusion of countries farther south do not, in general, apply. This neighbor-state, for example, resembles the United States more than most other American countries in suggestive respects: it stretches across the widest breadth of the continent from sea to shining sea; it shares the same— or roughly the same—majority language, has a similar economic profile, and mirrors the history of economic progress and political stability that is at the core of the self-image, cultivated in the United States, of America's "exceptional" nation. Our habit of treating the United States and Canada apart from the rest of the hemisphere is partly the result of a historical accident, partly the reflection of prejudice. For a relatively brief period in the nineteenth and twentieth centuries the history of the two most northerly countries in the Americas diverged, in some respects, from the rest. While the rest of the hemisphere got mired in preindustrial economics and predemocratic politics, the United States and Canada experienced, with relatively little disruption or dislocation, sustained growth, spectacular territorial expansion, rapid adjustment to changing global economic conditions, a high degree of political stability, and an exemplary record in the preservation and development of civil society. The results were startling. We live with them today.

Even the severest critic of the United States and the most romantic lover of the Latin has to acknowledge the difference: most American states oscillate between dictatorship and instability; not so the United States and Canada. Most American states find it hard to maximize their economic resources; not so Canada or the United States. One of the greatest problems of the history of the Americas is, why the divergence? One of the greatest unsolved problems of the future of the Americas is, what are we going to do about it? Those problems are the subject of this book. They can be fully understood, I believe, only by seeing the Americas whole.

A Pan-American approach cannot solve the problems, but it does put them into perspective. It suggests that divergence is either a brief and uncharacteristic episode in a common history or a predictable, containable effect of the essential plurality of a hemisphere always characterized by diversity, which has sometimes favored one region, sometimes another. It makes the present state of the hemisphere seem neither inevitable nor indefinitely sustainable. Gringo privilege is a product of history, not of fate. US hegemony is not the end of history, just another phase of unpredictable durability. If we want to be ready for future phases, we can and should replace our traditional ways of categorizing the hemisphere with others of more lasting validity.

BETWEEN COLONIZATIONS: THE AMERICAS' FIRST "NORMALCY"

The Americas started in the north. As far as we know, the first people in the hemisphere penetrated from the Old World where Asia nearly joins—and once did join—America, and spread southward from there. That is a fact, but as we shall see, the inferences generally drawn from it are false. Native American mythopoeia has generated objections, even on allegedly factual grounds. Indigenous origin-stories often include accounts of long migrations, but there are some that represent the ancestors as sprung from the earth their descendants inhabit. Apologists for land claims, or stake claimers for Native American priority over other human groups, have read these myths to mean that humankind originated here and that everyone else in the world is the product of colonizations that started in the Americas. There is no reason to believe their accounts. Nobody is autochthonous; the world was made by migrations. There never really was an Eden—a single place where humankind sprang into being—but Africa is, on present evidence, the nearest thing to a "cradle" of our species, where hominids lived for millions of years, humans very like ourselves for hundreds of thousands, and "modern humans"—*Homo sapiens sapiens*—for tens of thousands before the earliest inhabitants of the Americas.

For a long time the prevailing scholarly narrative of the first settlement of the Americas has begun in the last ice age. The earth tilted. The sun blazed. The ice cap slipped and spread. Glaciation sucked in vast volumes of sea. Across what is now the Bering Strait, the seabed was exposed. Toward the end of the period, according to the formerly dominant version, when a traversible gap opened between glaciers, a race of hunters crossed this land link to exploit a previously unhunted paradise. The abundance was such, and the animals so unwary, that the invaders ate enormously and multiplied prolifically. They spread rapidly over the hemisphere, hunting to extinction, as they traveled, the great game in which, in the Pleistocene era, the Americas abounded. This story appealed in an age of North American hemispheric hegemony; the spread of the hunters was like a dry run for manifest destiny. The "Clovis people," as they were dubbed after the name of an early archaeological site in New Mexico, seemed to preincarnate gringo virtues and skills: hustle and bustle, quick-fire locomotion, technical prowess, big appetites, irrepressible strength, prodigious cultural reach, imperial expertise, and a talent for reforging the environment.

By comparison, the truth about the peopling of the hemisphere is disappointingly undramatic. Though American archaeology is still really in its infancy, and too few sites have been excavated for a complete and reliable picture to emerge, evidence of human occupation is now available in so many places, scattered from the Yukon to Uruguay and from near the Bering Strait to the edge of the Beagle Channel, over so long a period, in so many different stratigraphic contexts, with such a vast range of cultural diversity, that one conclusion is inescapable: colonists came at different times, bringing different cultures with them. Asia and America were mutually accessible by land for long intervals over a period of maybe sixty thousand years, up to about ten thousand years ago; various groups could have crossed during one or more of those intervals. No generally accepted evidence dates any inhabited sites in the hemisphere earlier than about fifteen thousand years ago—the jury is out on some isolated claims of human artifacts more than thirty thousand years old—but even the most conservative assessment of currently available data dates the first arrivals during a time of very severe glaciation.

For much of the critical period, between about twelve and twenty millennia ago, barriers of ice obtruded, but—to judge from documented cases in the Old World or later in the history of the New—some migrant hunters like to keep close to the ice edge, where game is fattest. The first human intruders into the Americas probably came through corridors between walls of ice or along narrow, unglaciated shores, while seaborne migrations brought other arrivals and continued after the submersion of the land bridge. The catastrophic cluster of extinctions of around ten thousand years ago—which saw off the mammoth, the mastodon, the megahorse, the giant sloth, and the saber-toothed tiger, among at least thirty-five species of large fauna in the Americas—probably had something to do with new hunting techniques and perhaps with new hunting groups, but it can be understood only in the context of vast climatic changes that affected habitats and the whole ecological context on which the affected animals depended.

Many supposedly early finds of human habitation have proved to be delusions of overenthusiastic archaeologists—or, at least, unconvincing to impartial scrutiny. A few sites, however, are particularly striking because they constitute unanswerably strong evidence of the antiquity and ubiquity of settlement. Most of these are in the eastern United States—rather a long way from Asia and from the point at which the first populators entered the Americas but close to the world's most impressive concentration of modern schools of archaeology. Similarly, it is surprising how many important sites in the history of British archaeology are located within cycling distance of Oxford and Cambridge. Toward the mid-1970s, fifteen-thousand-year-old basketwork and fine-knapped tools emerged from deep under the discarded beer cans that topped a dig at Meadowcroft, on the Ohio River in Pennsylvania, near the border of West Virginia. Other similar sites are under investigation in the region between the Ohio and Savannah Rivers. Later in the same decade, excavations at Monte Verde in southern Chile revealed evidence preserved in a peat bog for about twelve and a half millennia: a twenty-foot-long wood-built, hide-covered dwelling with a big mastodon butchery and tool manufactory nearby. The inhabitants brought salt and seaweed from the coast, forty miles away, and medicinal herbs from mountains equally far in the opposite direction. Half-chewed lumps of seaweed preserve the image of the eaters' dental bites; a boy's footprints survive in the clay lining of a pit. This discovery stood the early history of the Americas on its head: the received story unfolded from north and south, but now the most impressive early culture—judged by material standards—had emerged in the far south, deep inside the South American cone.

If American history began in the north, a southerly location suggests two things about the people who occupied it: they were relatively long established in the hemisphere, and they were remarkably enterprising. Colonization that crosses climatic zones and adapts to radically unfamiliar environments is quite rare in history. Indeed, the prehistoric settlers of South America accomplished a stunning achievement, in this respect, in an impressively short time. Compared with people who stayed in the north, including the whole of what is now the United States, they were precocious in taking the first steps toward what we conventionally think of as civilization: producing food—instead of merely gathering it by hunting and foraging—and farming it, developing new species for their own needs.

In a cave called Tres Ventanas in the Chilca region of Peru, people were eating sweet potatoes about ten thousand years ago. No wild forms of the plant are known today, but if the Chilca varieties were produced by cultivation, they would be the world's oldest domesticated plants. Potatoes were being harvested in the same region from about seven thousand years ago. These must have been products of conscious planting strategies—the first authenticated agriculture of the Americas—for two reasons: first, because they are native to higher altitudes and must therefore have been transplanted; second, because they are developed from wild forms, which are smaller and contain higher concentrations of poisonous alkaloids (useful for deterring parasites but inconvenient for human consumers). These early potatoes, therefore, have to be the results of active selection by human hands.

No one knows how it happened. The magic that turned poisonous or indigestible plants into staples that could feed civilizations has inspired fantastic theories: myths that trace the techniques to Promethean heroes or divine benefactors; speculations that they were "diffused" from Old World civilizations by undocumented travelers. In fact, agriculture is a commonplace miracle that happened independently in widely separated places around the world, preceded and in part, perhaps, explained by a diversity of causes. Sometimes it was a consequence of abundance, which enabled people to experiment with planting and herding, or sometimes of stress, which compelled recourse to new techniques when populations rose or food supplies dwindled. Some cultivation began—it is reasonable to suppose—as a religious rite, as worshipers nurtured divine foods. Some was politically inspired, to supply chiefly feasts. Some happened by accident—or, to substitute a more convincing-sounding term, by coevolution; plants and animals evolved rapidly in and around human settlements, attracted by fertile waste dumps and middens, and humans appropriated the results. A common consequence was the interdependence of humans and newly emerging species: the development of plants that depended on human propagation, or animal food sources that could breed and survive only with human help. Foraging and farming are points along a single continuum, and the one sometimes grows into the other.

Early agronomy made the Andes and their environs a cradle of early civilization—of sedentary populations, thickly settled; of city building; of monumental art; and of early empires: powerful polities designed to regulate the storage and distribution of food, and constructed to wield wide sway over a variety of ecozones so that the products of different niches could be garnered against disaster. Precipitate mountains were a conducive environment because the topography of slopes and valleys enclosed a relatively large number of different microclimates within relatively short distances. In the most precocious zone, the ocean and the tropical forest are not far away on either side of the mountains. This is a region rich in biodiversity. Its earliest great monuments—vast earth mounds topped with stone-built chambers at Aspero, north of Lima, where little clay representations of pregnant women were buried by the builders inside the ceremonial spaces—are as old as the Great Pyramid and Sumerian ziggurats. Some sites of this era are located low on oceanside rivers, flowing down from the Andes, and are close to huge shell middens, which suggest that the inhabitants may have farmed mollusks for food, but most of them also seem to have imported tropical foodstuffs from east of the mountains, perhaps via highland sites, which evince the same sort of monumental architecture. Even these very early sites have yielded fragments of textiles and ceramics that foreshadow the aesthetic of all subsequent Andean civilizations: angular, highly abstract, with evocations of human and animal forms reorganized on a geometric grid, or beasts caught in moments of metamorphosis, as if in a shamanistic imagination.

Most of these experiments in civilization were short-lived; with modest technologies, they struggled to survive in capricious environments, where El Niño events caused tremendous fluctuations in weather conditions. They faced crises caused by their own success, when population levels crossed thresholds of unsustainability, or overexploitation impoverished their soils, or neighbors' cupidity unleashed wars. Their traditions, however, were renewable over time and communicable among a great variety of environments. The city of Chavín de Huantar, founded about three thousand years ago, demonstrated how prosperity and magnificence could be mobilized at middling altitudes in the Andes, using all the diversity of foodstuffs that a little world of microclimates could provide. Chavín became a regional cynosure, and its arts were models for all subsequent Andean civilizations. In the third century A.D. the city of Tiahuanaco—potato-fed, because its altitude, higher than Lhasa's, was hostile to grains—began to spread over a site of forty acres. For thirteen hundred years, until the Inca world collapsed, the effort to cultivate and build on a scale that defied nature was never entirely abandoned, and Tiahuanaco, as it gradually subsided into ruins, became a source of inspiration for all subsequent efforts. The Incas looked back to it in awe, rather as the Aztecs would to the ancient central Mexican metropolis of Teotihuacán— or, perhaps, as modern Mexicans look back to the Aztecs.

While primitive agronomy planted sweet potatoes and potatoes in the south, food production started independently in Mesoamerica—roughly, that is, modern Mexico and northern Central America—with the foodstuff that ultimately came to feed most of the Americas for most of history: maize. From weedy, spiky, humanly indigestible grasses, probably of kinds similar to those that still grow wild in the same region, the first edible varieties were in production at various sites around the Valley of Mexico by about 5000 B.C. The transformation, which produced the characteristically fat, many-grained cobs of the great Native American civilizations, was one of the triumphs of prehistoric food science. There is no evolutionary reason for maize to have such a structure. It came about as the result of purposeful selection and—probably—hybridization by cultivators. Processing, as well as production, demanded scientific flair, because maize needs proper preparation; untreated, it is a nutritionally deficient food, low in niacin. As a staple for huge populations, it could not compete with potatoes—which yield all the nutrients necessary for human life—without soaking when the grains were ripe, treating with lime or wood ash, removing the transparent skin, releasing the otherwise absent amino acids, and enhancing the protein value. Archaeological evidence of equipment for this process has been found on the southern coast of what is now Guatemala in sites from the mid- to late second millennium B.C.

Further or alternatively, maize eaters need supplementary foods, and indeed—for the early civilizations of much of northern, all of central, and parts of southern America— squash and beans formed with maize a "trinity" of divine plant foods wherever it was possible to provide all three in combination. The bottle gourd, the earliest known form of cultivated squash, was being pickled in Tamaulipas in the Sierra Madre of Mexico, and in Oaxaca (at the highly productive archaeological site of Tehuacán), as well as north of Lima in northern Peru and the Ayacucho Basin, long before the earliest evidence of maize cultivation.

For unknown reasons, the development of maize rapidly eclipsed that of potatoes and sweet potatoes in importance. Maize spread southward and northward. It became a useful supplement to native staples in Peru by about 3000 B.C. From about the middle of the second millennium B.C., new varieties proliferated in Mesoamerica as the result of systematic hybridization. It took a long time, however, to develop varieties that could succeed in all environments. In North America the crops on which early agricultural experiments were based were native to the region and ways of developing them were worked out on the spot. The confusingly named Jerusalem artichoke was first cultivated— or, at least, "managed"—in its native North American woodlands in the third millennium B.C. Other varieties of sunflower and sumpweed produced oily seeds. Goosefoot, knotweed, and maygrass could be pounded for flour. Squashes, which were indigenous to the same region, proved easy to adapt for agriculture. Maize spread into the region from the southwest in the third century A.D. but did not begin to transform the agronomy until about the end of the ninth century, when a new, locally developed variety with a short growing season became available.

The maize miracle was a mixed blessing. When it displaced native cultigens, maize did not make people live longer or stay healthier; on the contrary, the exhumed bones and teeth of maize eaters in and around the Mississippi floodplain bear the traces of more disease and more deadly infections than those of their predecessors. When Old World invaders adopted maize, they showed similar reluctance and even worse effects. Slaves fed on it suffered malnutrition through negligent preparation (see page 30). To the Iroquois, who became dependent on it, maize never lost its foreign flavor; they called wheat and maize by the same name. Wherever it took over, similar tyrannies accompanied it: collective effort to plant, harvest, process, and store it, and elites to organize its product and regulate its distribution. Soil had to be prepared in various ways according to the genus of place: earth might have to be ridged or raised; forest might have to be cleared. Surplus food demanded structures of power. Storage had to be administered, stockpiles policed. Entitlements had to be enforced. These activities have left ruins in the earth: the outlines of edifices, the rubble of cities, the fragments of artwork. Mass labor was mobilized in the service of mound building, fortification, religions of display, and the theatrical politics of rulers who demanded high platforms for their rites and specialized craftsmanship in the service of their propaganda and their magic.

Agriculture, in short, brought what we loosely call civilization, with its curses as well as its blessings. Even agriculturists who (as far as we know) stuck mainly to a diet of native seeds and squashes and lived in dispersed hamlets and individual farms developed in ways reminiscent of the maize cultivators. Some of them, too, created large earthwork precincts in geometrically exact shapes, luxurious ceramics, artworks in copper and mica, and what look like the graves of chiefly figures. It would be rash to suppose that all these developments were closely connected and dependent on a single "mother civilization" or point of diffusion. The connections that can be traced, however, all lead back to a relatively few places, to what we might call "centers of civilization" in the Americas. This is the beginning of the great trajectory of American history; the story of how and why parts of the hemisphere that, for most of history, nourished little life and unimpressive levels of material culture came to outstrip the old, rich productive centers; how regions apparently, for most of the past, under-endowed by nature and unconducive to civilization came to house a hemispheric hegemon and a global superpower. This story starts in the middle of the Americas.

THE CENTERS OF CIVILIZATION

In Mesoamerica the sequence of stunning experiments in civilization began, as far as we know, with the culture we loosely call Olmec. *Olmeca* literally means "rubber people" in Nahua, the indigenous lingua franca of central Mexico, where in precolonial times rubber for the ball game was imported from "hot lands" in the tropical south. Confusingly, art historians use the term "Olmec" to designate the rounded, supple aesthetic characteristic of many sculptural traditions of what is now southern Mexico, while also using it in the sense intended here, as the name of a civilization, original to what is now the province of Tabasco, of the second millennium B.C. More than three thousand years ago, the builders of the city of La Venta chose sites near mangrove swamps and rain forest, where they could exploit a variety of environments. Marshy lakes, full of aquatic prey, were alluring to settlers. Torridity and humidity cannot inhibit the civilizing imagination. Mounds for beans and squash, dredged from the swamp, became the prototypes for ceremonial platforms, ziggurats, and "pyramids." Canals for fish farming could be coaxed into a grid. By the end of the second millennium B.C., the city now known as San Lorenzo had substantial reservoirs and drainage systems, integrated into a plan of causeways, plazas, and artificial mounds.

The Olmecs have often been hailed as founders of the "mother civilization" of the Americas by believers in the diffusionist theory of civilization, which states, in brief, that civilization is such an extraordinary achievement that only a few gifted peoples can be credited with the inspiration for it, before it spread by example and transmission to other, less inventive peoples. This theory is almost certainly false; the Olmecs were part of a complex story of a constellation of civilizations emerging in widely separated places. Nevertheless, it seems undeniable that Olmec influence spread widely in Mesoamerica and perhaps beyond, working on communities already experiencing similar histories of their own.

The Olmecs' image is defined by huge sculpted heads, carved from stone and columns of basalt, each weighing up to forty tons, toted or dragged over distances of up to a hundred miles. Some have jaguarlike masks or squat heads with almond eyes, parted lips, and sneers of cold command—shaman rulers, perhaps, with the power of divine self-transformation. For the rites these figures suggest, the Olmecs built stepped platforms—ancestor types, perhaps, or maybe just early examples of the angular mounds and "pyramids" that became the typical monumental constructions of most indigenous civilizations of the New

World. Olmec rulers were buried in the disguises they affected in life—a caiman's snout, a jaguar's eyes—in pillared chambers, alongside the jade knives or stingray spines with which, presumably, they sacrificed their own blood in acts of propitiation of a kind also familiar in later indigenous traditions. *

After a "dark age" of diminished achievement, unilluminated by much evidence, civilization in the Olmec region resumed with the Maya, whose great era of city building and monumental art lasted from about the third to about the tenth century A.D. The Maya flourished in tropical lowlands and dense rain forests that seem, on superficial examination, so hostile to monument building; environments where work is toil, where soils are unstable, and where naturally occurring human foods are unplentiful. Yet the gleaming roof combs of Mayan temples still rise above the jungle in lowland Guatemala and Belize, announcing to the traveler, as their designers intended in their day, the size, wealth, and grandeur of the densely packed, intensely competing city-states—the allure of their markets, the deterrent of their armies. Mayan civilization, moreover, was adaptable to a variety of contrasting environments. With some modifications, it took to the abrupt highlands of Guatemala and the dry plateau of Yucatán almost as successfully as to the flat, wet lowlands.

The Maya evinced, in spectacular ways, some of the common threads of Native American civilizations from the Olmecs onward. Their societies were hierarchic and heiratic, ruled by elites whose distinguishing qualifications were prowess in war and access to the divine world. Their kings had shamans' power of communication with gods and ancestors; their portraits, engraved on slabs of stone and displayed in the grand plazas where their subjects assembled, show them in divine disguises or engaged in rituals of bloodletting designed to induce visions. They were sanguinary and competitive—competitive in trade and in war, which, for most communities, seems to have been almost constant. Wars were fought by terror; boasts of captives sacrificed are common in the texts. Scenes of sacrifice— including torturing to death and dismemberment alive— are fairly commonly depicted in the art.

Above all, the Maya were an urban people. Their polities were city-states, which sometimes engaged in territorial expansion and sometimes in close alliance but remained unimperial—they were too equipollent, perhaps, for that. The standard of life was urban: populations were dense and cities prolific. Everything important happened in the cities; the countryside was there to support and sustain them. Cities had nuclei of monumental buildings intended to house elites and display rites of divine propitiation and civic solidarity. These were surrounded by markets and thousands—sometimes many thousands—of peasants' impermanent dwellings of reeds and staves and a landscape adapted for intensive agriculture: small fields called milpas, carved or dredged between canals that were used for irrigation or fish farming. The fields were sown with the triad of native American staples: maize, beans, and squash, supplemented with other foods according to region or locality. Or they were devoted to cash crops, like the cacao that, as the source of the luxury beverage that accompanied rituals and feasts, was in high demand. In eighth-century Tikal—one of the biggest and most powerful cities in the Mayan constellation—a representation of a cacao pod was the symbol and naming glyph of King Ah Cacau, who, by converting the economy to cacao production, reversed an ecological crisis and economic decline. Today, when the sun is in the west and gilds the face of the huge temple where he was buried, you can still pick out the vast outline of his fading image, molded onto the temple façade.

The Maya possessed a singular feature—it is tempting to say "a secret ingredient"—because their writing system, the most expressive and complete known in the Native American world before the arrival of Europeans, did not spread to other culture areas and never formed part of the universal tool kit of pre-European civilization. Literature was the most evanescent of the pre-European arts. In some places, European state-makers or missionaries destroyed or suppressed it. In others, the means of transmission were purely oral. In others again, writing systems were ideographic or mnemonic and depended on reading techniques now lost. In yet others, the writings have never been decoded. The great exception is Mayan writing. Prolifically in lowland regions—though only very sporadically in the plateau and highlands—writings were confided to epigraphy, carved in stone and therefore able to withstand the ravages of wanton destruction and inevitable decay. Despite the depredations of overzealous missionaries in colonial times, who labored to expunge memories of paganism at the cost of destroying valuable old texts, a vast corpus of epigraphy survives, carved into the stones of the cities of the classic age from about the third to about the tenth century A.D. Heroic scholarship has gradually deciphered almost all of it.

Virtually all of it falls into two categories: first, records of astronomical observations and the arcana of priestly timekeeping—which was a vital area of interest in Mayan efforts to communicate with the cosmos and propitiate nature; second, dynastic records—the genealogies of kings, the records of their conquests, sacrifices, and acts of communion with their ancestors. On commemorative stelae and altars, on the façades of buildings, and in one case, at Copán in northern Honduras, on the reveals of a monumental stairway, the records of ruling dynasties—their wars, their alliances, their sacrifices to the gods—are transmitted in such detail, with such a wealth of meticulous chronological and genealogical information, that for the great age of Mayan epigraphy, from about the third to about the ninth century A.D., we are better informed about the political history of some Mayan states than we are about many European ones of the same era.

For lovers of creative literature, the range of the epigraphic material is perhaps disappointing. A single altar at Tikal contains what might be read as a poem; it is an account of a royal observation of a conjunction of Mars and Venus in the eighth century A.D., expressed in vividly evocative images. This is so small a literary legacy that scholars have often assumed that the Maya had no literature in the modern sense of the word—certainly, epigraphic records were not normally made of it. Yet an inkling of what has been lost emerges from a single precious text transcribed in colonial times. In 1688, Francisco Ximénez began his mission as parish priest of what is now Chichicastenango in the Guatemalan highlands. Parishioners whose confidence he won disclosed to him the existence of the "sacred book" of their tribe. Thanks to the bilingual edition he made of it, this work is the only surviving collection of ancient Mayan creative literature. Internal evidence dates its composition in its present form to the 1540s or 1550s, but it is rooted in earlier oral or glyphic tradition.

The core of the work is the story of twin culture-heroes, Hunahpu and Ixbalanqué, devotees of a cult com-

mon to all the civilizations of the Mesoamerican culture
area and to cultures influenced by them: the aristocratic
ball game, which was practiced both as an analogue of war-
fare and as training for war. Summoned to an away match
in the evil underground realm of Xibalbá, where the sinis-
ter lords are served by creatures of the night, the twins
prove unbeatable in a game enlivened by exciting ringside
commentary. The evil lords subject them to additional
tests in a series of torture chambers, where glowworms,
wasps, and jaguars help the twins survive. The twins engineer their own transformation by plunging into a pool—
to the deluded glee of the evil lords—from where they
emerge in the guise of poor conjurers. They entertain the
lords of Xibalbá to a mock dismemberment, not unlike
the modern conjurer's standby, sawing-the-lady-in-half. In
the mounting excitement, brilliantly evoked in the surviving version, the lords volunteer to take part in the act
themselves, with predictable results. Bereft of their leaders, the people of Xibalbá submit to the twins. The story
was famous throughout the Mayan world but never beyond
it, until European scholarship intervened.

Like the literature it encoded, the Mayan writing system did not spread along the trade routes that carried
other aspects of culture into central Mexico and, from
there, northward across the deserts and mountains into
what is now the United States. The system was designed
not so much to communicate as to keep secrets. It was an
esoteric code, so elaborate that it took long training to acquire, so arcane that only its initiates could interpret it to
the uneducated. Some features, especially the method of
recording numbers, did become widespread in Mesoamerica, less, perhaps, because of Mayan influence than because
the Maya had inherited them from a widely diffused Olmec

pattern. Other peoples had systems of their own, which met their own needs. Alongside carvings of butchered genitalia, undeciphered inscriptions, in a script that may well have a range of expression equal to that of the Maya, survive at Monte Albán, in the Valley of Oaxaca, where flourished and fought a civilization scholars call Zapotec, after the people who live there today. Most other Meso-american civilizations had picture writing—logographic or ideographic glyphs, which may not have been capable of expressing all the elements of a sentence or all parts of speech but that were good for recording data or serving as mnemonics for texts in ritual performance. Surviving examples show that before the conquest, these glyphs, written on deerskins or maguey paper, made of cactus pulp, were used for an impressive range of purposes.

Chronicles of Aztec conquests, and extensive Mixtec genealogies, read boustrophedon fashion, zigzag across the parchment. Tribute lists cover the Aztec empire, and divinatory and sacred calendars show when and what to sacrifice and define propitious and unpropitious birth dates. To judge from the way early colonial sources describe public readings by priests, armed with pointers, who would perform in front of divine texts, mythic and imaginative narratives could be sketchily committed to glyphs, and retraced and reconstructed, with the gaps supplied by memory, along elaborate patterns on the page. In early colonial times the same glyphic systems recorded place-names on maps and retold stories of tribal migrations in documents submitted to Spanish courts in pursuance of territorial claims.

Systems of this kind were not transmitted south from Mesoamerica. Andean civilizations had their own traditional methods of recording information, weaving symbolic patterns in textiles or, in the well-known Inca case, making quipus—knotting threads in ways that, according to the colors and shapes of the knots, conveyed meaning symbolically. Most modern authorities refuse to dignify this method with the name of writing, regarding quipus as repositories only of statistical data: census counts, fiscal records, tribute dues. According to the conventional wisdom, the Incas were arrested by illiteracy. A female novelist of the mid–eighteenth century offered one of the first demurrals: the plot of *Lettres d'une Péruvienne* by Françoise de Graffigny hinges on love letters written in quipus. In 1750 the scholarly Raimondo di Sangro, prince of Sansevero, defended her against learned derision, but his interpretation of quipu knots as a syllabary was denounced to the Spanish Inquisition, on the grounds that his doctrine was an apologia for paganism and barbarism. A few years ago the text on which Sansevero based his case came to light. It is a Jesuit work of the seventeenth century and its method of reading quipus seems at best fanciful and at worst fanciful; but the principle that knots are potentially as expressive as any other symbolic system of annotation is surely reasonable.

North of Mesoamerica, evidence of literate civilization before European intrusion is much harder to find. The first fully written language, as far as we know, in this part of the Americas was Cherokee, equipped in the eighteenth century with a syllabary inspired by, though not imitated from, European alphabets. Yet already in the seventeenth century Father Sagard, the missionary who explained the Huron to Europe, regarded them as potentially literate. He copied some of the inscriptions he saw engraved on trees, which recorded information about route finding and battle results—their whereabouts, the numbers killed and captured. Sioux pictograms in the nineteenth century could prompt beholders to recall wars, notable deaths, climatic fluctuations, memorable hunts, famines, and plagues. In many parts of North America, when Europeans first intruded, they found that people already made symbolic records of the world in the form of maps on bark and hide. Hernando de Soto's expedition through the southeast in 1539–1543 used indigenous maps as sources of intelligence for areas beyond its reach. An elderly local informant sketched the course of the Colorado River for Hernando de Alarcón in 1540; meanwhile, the landward branch of the same expedition collected a Zuni painting on skin of a group of settlements in the neighborhood of Hawikuh and sent it back to Spain. Informants "set down" a "report of all the country" of the Chesapeake for the Englishmen who landed in 1585. An Indian named "Nigual" made a surviving sketch map of New Mexico for Francisco Valverde in 1602. There were many similar cases, but they all seem to have occurred independently of one another. This raises a major problem: in a hemisphere of sundered cultures, how much "dependency" was there? To what extent did civilization in North America depend on what people there could learn from those to the south?

THE TRANSMISSION OF CIVILIZATION

Maps and pictograms remained the only documents made by people north of Mesoamerica. Nonetheless, although pre-European North America never learned writing from the civilizations to the south, city building and agriculture did spread northward. In these respects, Mayan civilization was equaled or outshone by some of the achievements of peoples of the Mesoamerican highlands. The biggest city in the pre-European Americas—and the probable inspiration of many others—was almost certainly Teotihuacán in the Valley of Mexico: eight square miles of stone buildings and causeways, six thousand feet above sea level, in the first century B.C. Huge pyramids and palaces conveyed an unmistakable sense of an imperial metropolis, where pilgrims or envoys from over a thousand miles away were housed. The inhabitants surrounded themselves with images still visible in decayed murals. Their sky was a feathered serpent who drooled fertility and sweated rain over blooming forests. Speaking birds uttered thunder. Coyotes dismembered screaming deer in an apparent analogy of sacrifice. Human sacrificers scattered blood from hands pierced by maguey spikes, or impaled human hearts on bones.

When Teotihuacán withered, for unknown reasons, in the eighth century A.D., a new metropolis arose, well to the southeast, at Tula, the "Garden of the Gods," where groves of stone pillars and ceremonial enclosures, irrigated by blood sacrifices, justified the name.

The site of Tula was abandoned in the twelfth century, but the ruins continued to inspire experiments in urbanization. By the time Cortés arrived in central Mexico, it was a world of hundreds of emulous city-states. The hegemonic community, Tenochtitlán, was the predatory center of a vast network of tributary relationships, which stretched across the breadth of the continent, from the Pánuco River in the north to what is now the Mexican-Guatemalan border in the south. To the awestruck Spaniards, the city recalled a grim fantasy: the abode of giants in a popular storybook. Cortés, perhaps exaggerating to impress readers back home, claimed that it was bigger and fairer than Seville.

North of the Aztec world there was nothing comparable. North America was relatively underdeveloped, partly because of a dearth of plant species capable of sustaining dense sedentary populations, until the arrival of maize. But the example of urban life did spread into what is now the United States, along with the trickle of culture, including corn, beans, squash, "irrigation, ceramic figurines, worked shell, earspools, copper bells, tripod palettes, ball-courts." Civilization—in as far as it happened at all—was fertilized from the south.

The roads north led across perilous territory. Nomadic peoples known collectively in Nahuatl as Chichimeca patrolled the northern edges of the Mesoamerican culture area, undertaking raids and depredations and, periodically, conquests, like those launched into China or Europe by steppelanders or into West Africa or the Mediterranean by Saharans. The Aztecs, according to one of their own origin myths, arrived in central Mexico as just such a nomad war band from the north, where the hostility of the inhabitants inhibited travel and trade. So did the rigors of the land, arid and mountainous. The high road north from what is now Mexico to the nearest patch of easily cultivable soil led through a sixty-one-mile pass known in colonial times as the *Jornada de la Muerte:* the march of death. In the early seventeenth century the poet-conquistador Gaspar Pérez de Villagrá described the route: rock-strewn defiles and dunes where the glare was so fierce that his eyes "boiled and bulged" and seemed to burst from their sockets, and men "breathed fire and spat pitch."

Yet the route was negotiable at need, sustained—from time to time, between discontinuities and disasters—through way stations of settled life. The most impressive of these, in the present state of archaeological inquiry, is Casas Grandes in Sinaloa, where the remains of a late-medieval warehouse for the macaw-feather trade bear witness to the northward transmission of Mesoamerican culture; macaw feathers were prized trappings of Mesoamerican aristocratic life, worn for the ball game and for war. Centers such as Casas Grandes probably linked up, in the twelfth century, with the road network that spread from Chaco Canyon, in what is now New Mexico. Urban life focused on enclosed ceremonial centers and meeting spaces, hollowed underground, in enclosed plazas, built over many generations to designs faithfully and unremittingly pursued. Apart from turquoise, which became the basis of a limited export trade, the region had little natural wealth, except for what could be coaxed from the ground by systematic agriculture and the adaptation of the Mesoamerican triad of staple goods, maize, beans, and squash. It was an impressive but ecologically fragile civilization, vulnerable to aggressors, with a history of faltering and ultimately of failure. Two hundred thousand trees were felled to construct Chaco Canyon.

It was harder still to ensure the onward transmission of Mesomerican crops and traditions beyond the world of Chaco Canyon. The prairie, though a flat expanse, was an ecological barrier, where there were few patches capable of sustaining sedentary life. Slow, uncertain processes communicated Mesoamerica's tool kit, food, and ways of life and thought across the prairie to the wetlands of the Mississippi or, perhaps, across the Gulf of Mexico, by seaborne trade, to the culture area associated with the mound-building civilizations of the North American Southeast. The mound-top rituals can be vividly reimagined with archaeology's help. A site in Georgia has yielded copper images of shamans in elaborate divine disguises—masked and winged, working up ecstasy with the aid of rattles fashioned from human heads. At some sites, wooden henges or sacred pergolas are still rotting away in place. At Spiro in Oklahoma, near the westernmost edge of this culture area, rulers approached their graves on massive biers, smothered in rich fabrics and shells and pearls from the distant ocean. Their retinues accompanied them as sacrifices, envisioning, drug-induced, the symbolically mutant creatures—winged spiders, antlered snakes, plumed wildcats—depicted on drinking vessels.

In the present state of our knowledge, the greatest city of precolonial North America was near the northernmost limit of Mesoamerican influence, on the unrivaled natural artery of the interior, the Mississippi, where routes of transmission from Mesoamerica via land and gulf converged. At its height, in the early thirteenth century, Cahokia probably had about ten thousand inhabitants; there were cities six or eight times that size in precolonial Mexico or Peru. Its central mound, though not high, was huge at the base: thirteen acres, as big as the biggest pyramid of Egypt. This was a self-important place, vying for attention, aiming for influence. The ultimate model that inspired Cahokia was some Mesoamerican capital—perhaps Teotihuacán itself. Carved symbols of the Mesoamerican-style agriculture that sustained it were buried under its temples: a snake with tails of gourd, goddess custodians of cornstalks.

Farther north, though city building was not attempted, maize reached as far as the climate permitted. Beyond the zone of 140 frost-free days a year, just north of Lakes Ontario and Erie, and along the southern shores of Lakes Huron and Michigan, the crop was not worth cultivating. Compared with the Mississippi floodplain and the warm south, civilization in the temperate and boreal forests was sustained by a different kind of ecology, which kept communities mobile and inhibited permanent settlement on a large scale. The forest was too precious to clear, except in small patches. The biggest towns, when Europeans arrived, were found among Iroquoian speakers in the Great Lakes region, which housed permanent communities of about a thousand people in longhouses of elm. The Iroquois proclaimed their fidelity to the forest every time they donned their ritual "false faces"—the disheveled, grimacing masks of the forest spirits whom they glimpsed in dreams or spotted between leaves, darting from tree to tree.

THE ENVIRONMENTAL MATRIX: DESERTS AND TROPICS

For most of history, the imbalance between the Americas, northern and southern, favored Mesoamerica and the Andes every bit as much as the modern imbalance favors the United States and Canada. The relative backwardness, the relative paucity of civilization in most of North America cannot be explained by isolation. The peoples of the Andes knew little or nothing, as far as we know, of those of Mesoamerica until Spanish conquistadores put them in touch with one another; that did not prevent civilizations from developing in the Andean region in parallel with those of Mexico and Central America. Nor is it merely a matter of the tyranny of geography; an impressive sequence of mountain civilizations, taking advantage of the different ecosystems provided by a world of slopes and valleys, microclimates, and diverse biota, took shape in the Andes. This contrasts with the absence of any comparable effort in the highlands of northern America, even though the Rockies presented, in one respect, a more favorable environment: they provided a habitat for a domesticable quadruped—the bighorn—that remained undomesticated. A great spine of mountains runs through the Americas from the Rockies to the Andes; mountains help to create favorable conditions of environmental diversity, because valleys cradle microclimates and different biota thrive at different altitudes, but for civilization to flourish, the Andes and the central Sierra Madre, close to rain forests, seas, and swamps for maximum diversity, are better placed than the mountains of the north.

In a similar way, though north and south in the American hemisphere have similarly arid deserts, the effort to civilize them encountered far more success in the south. One of the strangest deserts in the world is in northern Peru. Except in unpredictable years, when El Niño drenches the land, there is almost no rain, only a dry, gritty, almost nightly fall of sand. The region is cool, although only five degrees south of the equator, and dank with ocean fog. Little grows naturally, but modest rivers streak the flats, creating an opportunity to irrigate. The sea is at hand, with the rich fishing grounds created by the upwelling of the Humboldt Current and the mines of guano that could turn desert dust into cultivable soil. From the second century A.D. to the eighth, the civilization known as Moche made this desert rich with turkeys and guinea pigs, corn, squash, peppers, potatoes, and peanuts, which the people admired so much that they modeled them in gold and silver.

The civilization perished—literally, perhaps, washed away by El Niño. But another arose nearby, in the same region, after a few hundred years. The great city of Chan Chan was its capital; until the Inca destroyed it in the fifteenth century, it covered eight square miles and housed stores of maize, corrals of llamas awaiting butchery, security-conscious palaces, and workshops where goldsmiths worked imported precious metals. Farther south, the even more inhospitable desert of northern Chile proved civilizable to the people known as the Nazca roughly in the time of the Moche. They built subterranean aqueducts for irrigation to protect the water from the sun. Aboveground, they created some of the most ambitious works of art in the world: stunning representations of nature—a hurtling hummingbird, a cormorant with wings spread for flight, sinuous fish—and bold abstract designs—lines, triangles, and spirals—scratched in ocher deposits that film the rock. The rainless air has preserved them to this day. Some of the images are one thousand feet wide, too vast to be visible except from a height unattainable by the artists. These are works of godlike creativity, capable of keeping the imagination permanently aroused. By comparison, North American deserts stayed barren until modern times; the only comparable achievement was that of the Chaco Canyon people and their successors in parts of what are now Colorado, Arizona, and New Mexico, around the upper reaches of the San Juan, Salt, and Gila Rivers, between the eleventh and fourteenth centuries A.D.

Underlying these differences are inequalities of geography. For most of history, North America was doomed to be backward by the insufficiencies of the environment. A geographer from Mars would surely back the central and southern Americas for greatness against those of the north. Civilization is possible in almost every kind of natural environment, but in preindustrial times it always flourished best and endured for longest in areas blessed with environmental diversity: microclimates and a variety of habitats support healthy diets, energy surpluses, and reliable supplies. The shape of the American hemisphere therefore favors the south; the great breadth of the Americas is spread over the most inclement zones, in the far north, under unrelenting ice and snow. Although North America has a broad temperate zone, which an earlier generation of climatic determinists considered ideal for civilization, and the broadest part of South America is close to the equator, the conclusions usually drawn from these facts is false. In the equatorial south, a substantial zone is elevated above torrid altitudes; here arose the conspicuous civilizations of the Andes. Moreover, as the case of the Olmecs shows, tropical lowlands can be successfully adapted for civilized life without much in the way of sophisticated technology.

This is confirmed by another case, which deserves a moment's attention: that of the Amazonian lowlands. In 1542 the first Spaniards to navigate the Amazon claimed to have found densely populated states and towns of thousands of inhabitants, lining the river and inhabiting substantial wooden dwellings. These promising societies were fed by turtle and fish farms and extensive cultivation of bitter manioc, a food source with remarkable properties: it poisons vermin but, suitably prepared, nourishes humans. In one town the Spaniards found a fortified sanctuary, presided over by carved jaguars. In the art of carving, the Spaniards acknowledged native skill equal to that of European craftsmen. Yet these emerging civilizations disappeared with perplexing suddenness. The next Spaniards to navigate the Amazon, about twenty years later, saw nothing of the sort. It was as if scores of thousands of people had died or dispersed, and the river had devoured their dwellings. This is quite possible: European diseases, suddenly introduced in unimmunized communities, could have that sort of effect. By the time Francisco de Requena explored the frontier with Portugal for the Spanish crown in 1782, the Amazon was a byword for barbarism, full of intractable enemies and indomitable cannibals.

The accounts of the first Spaniards, long ignored as romance, are vindicated by current research. Moist, swampy environments suited early agriculture. Between eight and nine thousand years ago, at Peña Roja on the middle Caquetá in the Amazon Valley, "itinerant gardeners" felled trees and dug with hoes to plant squashes and a potato-like tuber resembling guinea arrowroot, which tastes like green maize. Papaya, manioc, and maize cultivars were known nearby by about 2700 b.c. In the "black earth" of the Amazon Valley, delicately modeled, finely decorated clay urns have survived intact since before the Spanish conquest; some finds date back to about a.d. 400. The mounds of Marajó, at the mouth of the Amazon, grew up from about a.d. 500; evidence of a marked population increase is visible in dense clusters of hearths and elaborately painted ceramics. The inhabitants boiled the bones of their dead, reddened the skeletons, and piled the bones in clay urns decorated with anthropomorphic reptiles. Symmetricality, intricacy, and order informed their aesthetic, until their civilization faltered for unknown reasons in about the mid–fourteenth century a.d.

Meanwhile, upriver, the Tapajó made an extraordinary range of fine pots, products of specialized, sacred craftsmanship, of which some examples, supported on anthropomorphic "caryatids," have cunningly worked handles in the form of vultures, or of caimans, frogs, monkeys, and birds, represented in a continuous flowing form.

For most of history the temperate parts of North America

presented far less favorable environments than the tropical forests of Brazil, for except on the frontiers of evergreen and deciduous species, temperate forests naturally sustain relatively few humanly edible plants, compared with tropical forests, and relatively fewer exploitable animal species. Some soils of temperate North America, moreover, are hard to cultivate. Under the historic forests, they tend to be thin and stony as one heads east from the middle and upper Mississippi.

THE DISTRIBUTION OF CIVILIZATION

Over the history of American civilizations as a whole, the nurseries and nerve centers have been in Mesoamerica—roughly speaking, that is, in what are now Mexico and a few countries to the south—and in the Andes or the adjoining lowlands. For millennia the great traditions of American civilization stuck to the same heartlands. Of such long-range influence as there was, most started from there. The Mesoamerican and Andean-centered theaters of endeavor had their limitations. Their civilizations did not last—but that did not inhibit the development of a genuine civilizing tradition. Their reach was short and they knew little or nothing of one another, but their influence seemed to spread nonetheless.

In North America, cultures that made contact with the great civilizations of the south fell under their spell and imitated their models. For instance, the methods of food production and city building that drove civilization forward in the north tended to be patterned on those of Mesoamerica. It is probable—though the evidence is equivocal—that Andean models had a similar influence on the development of intensive farming and settlement in the Amazon Valley in precolonial times. In general, southern superiority, northern inferiority was the normal pattern of the precolonial history of the Americas. "Normalcy" comes and goes; it may recur but it does not necessarily last forever. How much longer did—could—this precolonial normalcy last once the changes instigated by European intrusions began?

COLONIAL AMERICAS: DIVERGENCE AND ITS LIMITS

THE ABIDING SUPREMACIES

The modern story of the Americas is one of transition from north-on-south to south-on-north dependency. At the heart of that story is the late emergence—against the long run of history—of a hegemonic state, which became a superpower, in the north. In the colonial period these changes were foreshadowed and in some respects begun— but only, I mean to argue, slowly and imperfectly. New forms of civilization emerged, of European origins or influence, and the old centers in Mesoamerica no longer provided unique models for peoples farther north. Still, the areas that had formerly housed the great civilizations of the Americas continued to do so in colonial times. The biggest cities, the greatest wealth, the densest populations, the most conspicuous achievements in art, thought, and science were still concentrated where the traditional indigenous civilizations had flourished. In colonial times American disparities seemed to favor areas colonized from Spain and Portugal.

The Iberian colonies had a head start. The first of them was founded by Columbus on Hispaniola on his second transatlantic voyage in 1493. In an extraordinary half-century of expansion, the Spanish monarchy acquired, by conquest or diplomacy, the richest, most populous, most easily exploitable, and by conventional standards most civilized regions of the hemisphere, including the whole of the Mesoamerican and Andean culture areas. The former empires of the Aztecs and Incas, which in the early sixteenth century were among the most rapidly growing and ecologically diverse states in the world, were virtually swallowed at a gulp. Traditionally this unprecedented intercontinental empire has been represented as the fruit of feats of arms by godlike Spaniards whom natives are supposed actually to have mistaken for gods. In reality, the process was more insidious, more durable, and more believable than any mere feat of arms: the monarchy grew by accommodation with existing elites, by exploiting indigenous rivalries and securing indigenous collaborators. That was how a relatively poor, unpopulous, and peripheral European power came to establish so privileged a position of command in so much of the Americas.

By the end of the sixteenth century—before the French or English had established a single enduring colony anywhere in the hemisphere, the Spanish monarchy in the New World effectively included all the biggest and most productive islands of the Caribbean and a continuous swathe of territory from the edge of the Colorado plateau in the north to the River Bío-Bío in southern Chile; it extended from sea to shining sea across the narrow reaches of the hemisphere, and along the Atlantic coast of what is now Venezuela, with a southerly corridor to the Atlantic, across what is now Bolivia and along the Paraguay and River Plate. In most areas that the Atlantic wind system made easily accessible from Europe, Spain had preempted potential rivals, except on the Brazilian coast, where, by agreement with Spain, Portugal had a series of sugar-producing colonies. The relatively late start made by other colonizers and would-be colonizers, and in particular by the English and French monarchies, was not the result of any inherent inferiority on their part; the best portions of the hemisphere were in other hands, and only the dregs were left. It took a long time to find the will and ways to exploit them.

Outside areas of Spanish control, regions of sparse population could not easily be exploited for new forms of production without large quantities of slaves from the only big reservoir of such labor: Africa. For the first century and a half or so of the colonial era, Spanish naval supremacy and Portuguese control of many of the sources of slaves denied adequate supplies of this resource to the non-Iberian colonies. Except in the Caribbean, where sugar would grow on islands seized from or rejected by Spain, it was hard to find crops suitable to sustain colonial life; tobacco was the first, introduced into Virginia in 1614. Later in the century, rice made fairly large-scale settlement practical in the Carolinas. It was always possible for independent farmers to found smallholdings for their own subsistence, as they did with remarkable success even in the inhospitably rocky soils of New England from the 1620s. But this form of exploitation could never be the foundation of prosperity. New England only really began to reveal its potential as a great world center of wealth and civilized life in the eighteenth century, not because of its own resources but because so many of the inhabitants took to the sea; like classical Greece and ancient Phoenicia, it became a maritime civilization, making up for the poverty of its home soils by trade and the exploitation of marine resources.

Though explorers scoured unfrequented regions of the Americas for natural resources in the late sixteenth and seventeenth centuries, major sources of gold, silver, pearls, and precious gems remained a Spanish monopoly until the opening up of the Brazilian interior toward the end of the period. The areas left for the English and French to exploit contained only fool's gold, such as the iron pyrites found by Martin Frobisher in Canada in 1576, which deceived investors into ruin and lured adventurers to their deaths. Furs were the "black gold" of the far north, and south of beaver habitat, deerskins represented, in a more modest degree, a similar luxury product. But, like the timber and fish that also abounded in and around North America, resources of these kinds could not alone sustain permanent or populous colonies: for this *coureurs des bois,* migrant merchants and hunters, as well as seasonal visitors were needed.

For most of the sixteenth and seventeenth centuries there was only one other attraction for Europeans in North America, and it was of very limited appeal. The indigenous inhabitants, who, from most perspectives, were a disincentive to settlement, were a magnet for missionaries. "Come over and help us," said the Indian on the seal of the Massachusetts Company. On the whole, however, missionizing was a rare vocation in Protestant Europe. With few exceptions, only Catholic religious orders had enough manpower and zeal to undertake it on a large scale, and outside areas of Spanish rule their efforts were disappointing. The Huron became, in the seventeenth century, the shining example of indigenous receptivity to the gospel, but—in combination with wars against neighboring, pagan communities— the diseases the missionaries imported wiped out almost the entire people.

The most vivid mark and measure of success in the colonial world were its cities. As soon as Columbus returned from his first voyage and news of America began to circulate in Europe, engravers imagined what they called the Indies filled with magnificent cities. In areas of Spanish rule, it was a vision quickly realized, for Spanish imperialism was uncompromisingly urban-minded. When two Englishmen meet on a savage frontier they found a club; two Spaniards in the same circumstances found a city. Spanish colonization slotted into the existing framework of indigenous civilizations; in an extraordinarily productive period of expansion in the 1520s and 1530s, while the existing great urban centers of Mesoamerica and the Andean region were absorbed into the Spanish monarchy by conquest or diplomacy, the biggest cities of the Americas acquired new characteristics: Spanish-speaking elites, new indigenous bourgeoisies who served Spaniards' economic needs, a black slave class for domestic service, Spanish courts and town councils, Christian religious foundations, cathedrals, and even—in Mexico City—a university and a printing press. A new aesthetic of arches and arcades and proportions fixed by the Golden Number smothered the old angular look of indigenous architectures. Some old cities were flattened and rebuilt, others lightly adapted and recrafted; some were abandoned as a terrible demographic crisis unfolded—collapse of the indigenous population, caused by the unfamiliar diseases the new arrivals brought with them. Some indigenous capitals were replaced with new cities on new sites, like Lima, still perhaps the most Spanish of Spanish-American cities in looks and atmosphere. The civic model of life, the city-centered model of administration, was extended into new areas. From the 1570s, the Spanish crown issued meticulous regulations for the construction of new cities, with their grid plan and classical aesthetics and monumental scale, the preordained placing of cathedrals and seats of secular administration, their hospitals and schools. The archives are full of the plans of projected cities, and many of them were actually built. But in North America in the seventeenth and early eighteenth centuries, beyond the Spanish frontier, cities of English and French construction generally remained, in a sense, in the Iroquois tradition: they were built largely of wood and, though intended for permanent occupancy, had a gimcrack air of instant dereliction.

So Mesoamerica and the Andes remained preponderant in resources and attainments. Unsurprisingly, therefore, the colonial societies of the north lived, for most of the period, in awe of those of the south—envying their gold and silver, imitating their plantations and ranches, emulating their cities, coveting their territory but fearing their further expansion. English conquistadores, for instance, aped those of Spain. The first instructions to the colonists of Virginia ordered them to maintain a pretense of divinity in dealing with the natives, and to conceal any white men's deaths in order to project an image of immortality. This was naïve. It was based on a mythical version of early Spanish conquistador success, according to which the Aztecs had mistaken Cortés for a god or a divine representative. In fact, the Aztecs were unsusceptible to such nonsense. They were an inland people, with no traditional legends of "gods from the sea." It was the Spaniards who had a godlike perception of themselves and Cortés who put the myth into Aztec mouths, in an attempt to claim that they had voluntarily resigned their sovereignty into his hands. Captain John Smith, the most dynamic leader of early Virginia, was a voracious reader with a storybook self-image, who, I believe, modeled himself on Spanish predecessors. He claimed—in imitation of a story Columbus told about himself in Jamaica—to hold Indians spellbound by his knowledge of cosmography. Smith also applied methods apparently modeled on Cortés's, using terror and massacre to keep Indians cowed and trying to exploit a special relationship with the natives' paramount in order to rule though him.

The real maker of success in Virginia was John Rolfe, who borrowed from Spanish examples the two ingredients of his formula: first, he was the husband of Pocahontas—the forger of a kind of understanding with the natives, based on collaboration, mutual benefit, and carnal alliance, which was normal in Spanish colonies but remained unfortunately rare in English colonial practice. Second, he introduced "Spanish tobacco" from the West Indies, which became Virginia's monoculture, the large-scale export crop that turned the colony from an unprofitable swamp into a field for settlers. It was farmed at first mainly with a form of forced labor imported from England—"indentured" poor, escapees from social exclusion at home—but there were never enough of these, and as the market for black slaves gradually opened up to the English, Africans replaced them. Again, the model of exploitation was found in the Spanish, Portuguese, and (by now) Dutch colonies to the south.

From Virginia southward, English North American colonies naturally—literally, naturally—resembled those already exploited in Mesoamerica and South America by Spanish, Dutch, and Portuguese investors. They were hot and wet, with torrid lowlands that could be adapted to planting cash crops with the labor of imported slaves. When tobacco reached Virginia, it had to be a West Indian variety, because the native tobacco was unsmokeable to European palates and thus unsalable in Europe. The first English-run sugar industry in Barbados was directly copied from the Dutch enterprise in Pernambuco, with Dutch capital and savoir faire. The effects on settler society were predictable.

Economic reliance on large-scale, capital-intensive enterprises created huge disparities of wealth. English planters
in North America and the Caribbean resembled Spanish
hacenderos. A society of *latifundiae* grew up, more reminiscent of the Mediterranean or Brazil than of England or
New England. In 1700, half of one county in Virginia was
owned by the top 5 percent of settlers by wealth.

After experiments with other kinds of enforced labor,
slavery became the universal method for developing the
plantation crops, including the rice and cotton that, in
preference to tobacco and sugar, suited some of the land
the English seized. The system was imitated from Spanish
and Portuguese precedents in areas where native labor suffered depletion or evinced intractability. It was driven by
climate, as is apparent from the failure of early antislavery
statutes in Georgia; subtropical America could not be
made to pay without labor from Africa. Nowhere else
could supply, in sufficient numbers, workers adaptable to
the climate. In slaving imaginations slavery represented a
civilizing process, the recovery of one of the virtues of the
ancient Greek and Roman worlds, which slave energy had
fueled. In actuality, it is hard to imagine a practice more
corrosively barbarizing. Slavery nourished its own forms of
mendacity and cant: racism, which represented blacks as
inherently inferior to whites or purported that they were
better off enslaved than at home. It corrupted owners by
giving them power over the lives and bodies of their slaves
and encouraging them to abuse it. It corrupted shippers,
who overcrowded their cargoes to maximize their profits
and, in verifiable incidents, tossed blacks overboard for the
insurance. It kept blacks and whites in mutual fear and
loathing, driving black rebels to horrific and despairing ex-
pedients for refuge or revenge, and trapping colonial gov-

ernments in policies of inhuman rage and repression. It let
loose predatory gangs of slavers and bounty hunters. It encouraged war in Africa between raptor states, which prof-
ited from the trade, and their victims.

The moral effects are important because every memory
of inhumanity is precious in a world still riddled with vices
of cruelty and greed. For our immediate purposes, however, slavery is relevant because it was a common American experience, covering both "Anglo" and "Latin" zones.
From Virginia to Bahía, much of Atlantic-side America
became, in early colonial times, a world that was almost
uniform in one respect. It was a world "slaves made," more
African than European. Africans were predominant in
numbers. They practiced their own religions, spoke their
own languages, maintained their own household patterns,
and ate their own food. Their African culture was only
very slowly transformed, because most owners resisted
evangelization of their slaves; the Bible might give them
subversive ideas about the equality of men; clergy might
interfere with owners' rights of abuse.

As well as African ways of life, there were African polities, independent states established by runaways, sometimes in collaboration with indigenous peoples. The most
successful maroon kingdoms achieved recognition by colonial authorities. It was easier to establish a modus vivendi
than run the risks of war and the inflammation of slaves'
grievances. The best-known case is that of the maroon
kingdom of Esmeraldas in the Colombian hinterland, which
was accorded a treaty by the Spanish crown in 1599; the
viceroy commissioned a commemorative painting from
Alonso Sánchez Galves, the best painter in the colony at
the time. It shows the maroon leader and his sons, sumptu-
ously attired as Spanish gentlemen but bejeweled with

gold African- or indigenous-style ear and nose ornaments. Beyond British colonies, in the seventeenth and eighteenth centuries, there were maroon states in Carolina and Jamaica, protected by agreements with the colonial authorities that guaranteed their peaceful toleration in exchange for joint regulation of the fate of new fugitives from the plantations. In the Surinamese backcountry, a maroon state was established in 1663 (the year the maroons of Jamaica received the first treaty acknowledging their autonomy), with the connivance of planters who sent their slaves there to evade the head tax due on them. The best-documented and longest-lasting of the runaways' polities was upcountry from Pernambuco, where the kingdom of Palmares defended its independence for almost the whole of the seventeenth century. At its height, under King Zumbi, it had a royal guard five thousand strong, a court life elaborate enough to impress visiting Portuguese, and a black elite rich enough to have large numbers of slaves of their own.

COLONIAL RELIGIONS

Even in religion—which is usually thought of as a great point of divergence between the moieties of the Americas in colonial times—there was more imitation than one might at first suppose. The French in Canada tried to use missionaries as front-liners, rather as the Spaniards did in Florida, New Mexico, and Yucatán. Religious uniformity, enforced by persecution, was a standard set by the Spanish Crown in its own colonies and echoed in most of the early colonial Americas. One of the most cherished myths of the people of the United States is that freedom of conscience was the foundation of their tradition of civil liberties. Yet

Puritan Massachusetts wanted a Puritan state, from which heretics would be excluded and in which dissidents would be silenced, much as Spain wanted a Catholic state in Spanish America. In states where toleration did begin to flourish in the seventeenth century, it was as a result of the outflow of refugees from Puritan intolerance enriching the populations of Rhode Island, founded as a refuge for Baptists, and Pennsylvania and Maryland, which were established for Quakers and Catholics respectively. American religion is supposed to deliver the blessings of idealism without the discomforts of clericalism, but godly little tyrannies are still on the statute books in every state.

In any case, sectarian historical traditions have ludicrously exaggerated, or actually invented, the cultural differences between Protestantism and Catholicism. Of course, *odium thelogicum* was a powerful influence on the mutual perceptions of colonists from different parts of Europe, which, at the relevant time, were developing mutually hostile religious traditions. And of course, Catholic missionary efforts proved more committed and sustained than those of Protestants. Crucial similarities, however—"common differences"—balance and in some respects outweigh these divergences.

The greatest common difference colonial societies made to the religious history of the Americas was that they all introduced Christianity. The forms of Christianity that became characteristic of Spanish America were every bit as heterodox, in their way, as the Protestantism of most of the English colonies. In part, this was because of the imperfections of the "spiritual conquest." Missionaries were few; cultural and linguistic obstacles impeded communication. Evangelization was scanty, especially in the early days, when Franciscan missionaries, urged on by their sense that the last days of the world were at hand, practiced mass baptisms preceded by minimal catechesis. Pre-Christian religion was probably ineradicable. In partial consequence, Latin American Catholicism is rippled, to this day, with indigenous features.

Secular scholars, and Protestant critics of Catholic evangelization, call these "syncretic" features or "pagan survivals." It is hard to resist this opinion; indeed, it was shared by many missionaries in the colonial era. In central Mexico, in the mid–sixteenth century, the church was convulsed by fears that new cults disguised pagan practices; doubts arose even concerning the purity of the veneration of Nuestra Señora de Guadalupe herself—the apparition of Our Lady, supposedly to an Indian shepherd boy on the site of a pre-Christian shrine, that had demonstrated the sanctity and grace of Mexican soil in the 1530s. In 1572 one of the worst recorded cases of missionary violence erupted in Yucatán, when the head of the Franciscan mission became convinced that some of his flock were harboring idols. The reports that alerted him came from native informants, motivated, probably, by traditional hatred and rivalry between indigenous communities rather than by any zeal for the facts. In the subsequent persecution, thousands of Indians were tortured and 150 died.

A similar case occurred in Huarochirí, Peru, in 1609, when a parish priest was condemned for using excessive violence toward backsliders among his flock. The papers he collected include the story of a revealing trauma. Don Cristóbal Choque Casa, the son of a local notable and community leader, reported that, some thirty or forty years after his people had been nominally converted by a vigorous Jesuit mission, he was on his way to an amorous assignation at the abandoned shrine of a tribal god when he was assailed by the devil in the form of a bat. He exorcised the spot by reciting the Lord's Prayer in Latin and the following morning summoned his fellow natives to warn them not to frequent the shrine on pain of being reported to the parish priest. But that same night he was afflicted with a dream in which he was irresistibly drawn to the accursed spot himself and compelled to make a silver offering to the god. The story evokes a vivid picture of the consequences of "spiritual conquest": old shrines, so neglected that they are fit only for bats and fornicators; abiding powers, so menacing that they can still haunt the dreams, even of a sinner sufficiently indoctrinated to be able to say the Pater Noster in Latin.

For the rest of the colonial period the eradication of pre-Christian devotions in Peru became the work of professional "extirpators." In most of the rest of the Spanish American world, every new generation of clergy repeated the frustrations and disillusionment of their predecessors: the Indians seemed unable to forget their old rites of the propitiation of nature. I recall how, a few years ago, I almost became convinced of the theory that colonial religion was "syncretic" in a museum in Guatemala City, as I gazed at a seventeenth-century indigenous artist's painting of the Virgin and noticed that the frame, though carved with every swirl and curlicue one would expect of a baroque hand, actually represented a Chaac mask—the face of the so-called rain god of the preconquest era. Yet the proper comparison for colonial religion is not—or not solely—with the religion of the indigenous past but with that of the Europe of the same era, where clerical bafflement at the intractability of "popular" religion was every bit as great. Europe, in godly eyes, was another Indies, full of underevangelized people in rural fastnesses or rootless towns. The Christianity of the American countryside was deficient in similar ways to that of the European countryside, warped by anxiety for survival in this world from proper concern about salvation in the next. Rites to induce rain, suppress pests, elude plague, and fend off famine drove Scriptures and sacraments into neglected corners of ordinary lives. As the early modern period unfolded, and the Reformation and Counter-Reformation took effect, clergy and educated laity acquired ever-higher standards of doctrinal awareness, ever deeper experiences, of Christian self-consciousness. Their expectations of their flocks increased accordingly, which accounts for the continual renewal of their dissatisfaction. Meanwhile, there was as much variety in the Christianity of Indians in Spanish America as in that of Europeans in Anglo-America.

Black religion—though it varied a lot from place to place, molded into conflicting traditions by the influence of Protestantism and Catholicism respectively—always had one thing in common: it was always black. Brazil is the best-documented area and has, in this respect, I think, a characteristic profile. Here, in colonial times, black artistic vocations and religious devotion were alike centered on cult images. Black confraternities often paid for them. These were vital institutions for colonial society generally, melding the deracinated, renewing their sense of identity and belonging. They were even more important for blacks, who were compulsory colonists, traumatically transferred to an alienating environment. Confraternities cushioned and comforted them in a white man's world: volatile organizations, "created and dissolved with extraordinary rapidity," as one of their most distinguished historians has said. Overall, however, they kept on growing. In Salvador in the early eighteenth century, six black brotherhoods of Our

Lady of the Rosary were officially recorded, and five more exclusively for mulattos; by 1789, eleven new black confraternities had joined them. Over the same period in Rio, the number of such associations nearly trebled.

Encouraged by the church, and especially by the Jesuits and Franciscans, the black brotherhoods were incorrigibly subversive. For the guardians of the colonial power structure, their choice of celestial patrons, whom they paraded through the streets and elevated in shrines, was often self-assertive, sometimes defiant. Saint Elesbaan, for instance, was a warrior-avenger, a black crusading emperor of Abyssinia who led an expedition to avenge the massacre of Christians by a Jewish ruler in Yemen in 525—easy to reinterpret as a symbol of resistance to *converso* capitalists. The Jesuits who promoted his cult probably knew only the Byzantine version of his legend, which misrepresented him as a model of Christian orthodoxy who supposedly became a hermit after sending his golden crown as an ex voto to Jerusalem. Benedict of Palermo, perhaps the favorite patron of black confraternities, achieved huge popularity on his beatification in 1743. Born the son of slaves in 1543, he became a hermit in his youth to escape taunts about his blackness; then, as a Franciscan, he rose to become guardian of his friary and work miracles after his death. Saint Iphigenia was an apocryphal black virgin, whom Counter-Reformation scholars unearthed from sixth-century texts, the purpose of which was to represent the conversion of Ethiopia as an achievement of apostolic times. She was supposedly the king's daughter, who, rejecting a proposal of marriage from her father's successor, resisted the spells of her suitor's magicians with the help of two hundred fellow virgins. Priests favored her cult because she embodied the triumph of faith over magic, to which blacks were supposedly susceptible. But it had its subversive aspect, too, sanctifying virginity in a slave society where women wished sterility on themselves. Veneration of the Mother of God was closer in spirit to the fertility religions supposedly traditional among migrants from Africa and more consistent with the interests of slave owners, who wanted their human livestock to breed. Black Catholicism was an excitant, not an opiate. A commonly depicted scene was of white Judas, tortured in hell by black tormentors. Among the demands of black rebels in 1798 was equality of treatment for black and mulatto confraternities.

Colonial-period black Catholicism really was different from that of whites. Masters excluded slaves from mass, ostensibly "on account of the smell" but really to keep them out of the hands of dangerously radical clergy. White confraternities reviled blacks "with their guitars and drums, with their mestizo prostitutes" and with their revolutionary pretensions, "just as though they were no different from honest white people." Fugitive blacks who set up their own backwoods communities and independent kingdoms were formally excommunicated; the hierarchy usually refused their requests for chaplains. Evangelization in Brazil began before the Counter-Reformation, when the clergy were still content with superficial levels of indoctrination. It continued in an era of growing Catholic sensitivity to the native heritage of potential converts, who were not always called on to abjure all their culture in order to become Christians. The mulatto priest António da Vieira, who became a royal chaplain, imported "masks and rattles to show the heathen that the Christian religion was not sad." In partial consequence, Brazilian Catholicism is an umbrella term for a bewildering range of styles of devotion, with diverse and deep—dare one say racial?—roots. "Catholicism superimposed itself on the African religion rather than replacing it," said Roger Bastide, who devoted his life to studying the effects. Missionaries among the slaves practiced "the illusion of catechesis," according to Brazil's great sociologist of religion, Nina Rodrigues. What was borrowed from Christianity was not doctrine but disguise—"camouflage," some say, in which paganism has eluded persecution. As the macumba priestess María José explained, slaves replaced images of the Toruba god Orixa with statues of Christ, "and the Portuguese thought, 'What wonderful slaves, all they do is pray to Jesus Christ!' " So black religion was distinctive and—from a clerical point of view—deficient. Outside the Iberian colonies—and especially in those of the British and Dutch, where plantations were inaccessible to religious orders—underevangelization was even more marked.

As for the religion of white Americans in colonial times, its great common—albeit not constant—feature was enthusiasm. Its most characteristic manifestation was, perhaps, the "Great Awakening" of evangelical revivals in the British colonies during the mid–eighteenth century; a reaction against religious rationalism made popular idols of fervent preachers like Jonathan Edwards, whose purpose was "not to store heads but stir hearts." "Outcries, faintings, convulsions and such like" replaced liturgy, as critics complained, among congregations "seriously, soberly and solemnly out of their wits." This was indecorous, but it was hallowed by enthusiasm. It had no exact counterpart in Catholic worship, though charismatic preaching and emotional exhalations from the congregation were encouraged in a parallel movement in the eighteenth-century Catholic world. The enthusiasm that inspired it, had, however, close resemblances in the Spanish parts of the Americas.

For the first colonies of most of the European powers were founded at an exciting time in the history of European Christianity: an era of evangelization. Catholic clergy and Protestant divines were engaged—for all their differences—in a common project: spreading enhanced Christian awareness, catechizing underevangelized flocks in neglected rural solitudes and new urban wens, where the medieval church had been absent or inert. Many colonies were formed or infiltrated by refugees from religious persecution, who took their faith seriously: Catholics and radical Protestants in North America, Judaizers in Iberian colonies. Even hardheaded laymen could prove amenable to religious enthusiasm in the heady atmosphere of a New World where everything seemed possible and a new church might be constructed from scratch, without the corruption and distortions that had warped Christ's teaching in the Old World. Columbus and Cortés—neither of whom evinced much interest in religion in their early lives—both had visions of a restored apostolic age in the lands they conquered.

The most extreme form of enthusiasm, millenarianism, is in some ways the characteristic religiosity of the Americas. It can be detected in pre-Christian indigenous religions— in central Mexico, most peoples celebrated rites of renewal of the earth in fire every fifty-two years and nourished myths of the periodic immolation of the world in a divine furnace. But for these and other indigenous cultures we know about, time was cyclical. Every immolation was the start of a new cycle. The end of time—as Christians imagined it, the climax of linear progress—was strictly unimaginable. Franciscan utopians introduced Christian millenarianism to the

New World in the sixteenth century. Most of the early missionaries came from a few Franciscan houses in Andalusia, where a particular tradition within Franciscanism, known as the Spiritual tradition, was nurtured. Its main thrust was for the preservation of the founder's spirit, rather than formulaic or pharisaic adherence to rules. Strong within Spiritualism, however, was a prophetic mind-set, imported into the order owing to the influence of a twelfth-century Sicilian abbot who pioneered the use of the Bible for divination. His followers were obsessed with the imminence of the end of the world, which, they thought, would be preceded by the dethronement of the Antichrist in a cosmic war, inaugurating the "Age of the Holy Spirit."

Ever after, chiliastic fantasies turned heterodox minds mad at frequent intervals—more regularly, I think, in the New World than in the Old. Lope de Aguirre imagined himself as the embodiment of God's wrath. His Franciscan contemporary Fray Francisco de la Cruz was the self-proclaimed universal pope and emperor of the last days. The Spirituals' fervor mingled with whatever predisposal to millenarianism was inherited from indigenous tradition. In Mexico in 1541 a Nahua chief called Don Martín Ocelotl proclaimed the Second Coming, incarnate in himself. In 1579 in Paraguay a Guaraní chief, Oberá the Resplendent, launched a rebellion with a similar message. In Peru so-called Inkarrí movements kept phantasmagorical memories of the Inca empire alive throughout colonial and into modern times and fused them with expectations of the coming of a "Last World Emperor."

Messianic language has been common in Latin American political rhetoric. Simón Bolívar, Augusto Cesar Sandino, Victor Raúl Haya, Abimael Guzmán (the archterrorist of the Sendero Luminoso movement), and hundreds of lesser figures have all been hailed inaugurators of the millennium. In the convictions of his hero-worshipers, the Mexican peasant revolutionary Emilio Zapata "will return" from the grave, like Arthur or Charlemagne or Christ, to renew the world.

Meanwhile, North America inherited similar traditions, supplemented by the original forms of millenarianism that grew up in Protestantism. Because millenarianism was generally considered heretical or was associated with heresies, even in Protestant environments, it became common in America, driven there by persecution, nourished there by toleration. Anabaptism, world's-end biblical fundamentalism, and sects invented by chiliasm-crazed prophets have all been formative influences in the making of the United States. The founders of Massachusetts envisaged a refuge for those God intended "to save out of general destruction." John Cotton predicted the End would come in 1655. Increase Mather felt he could hear God's "murdering pieces go off" as he watched the comet of 1680. The Shakers called themselves "the United Society of Believers in Christ's Second Coming." The Adventists, Mormons, Jehovah's Witnesses, Ghost Dancers, and hundreds of other sects who have kept millenarianism alive in the centuries since independence have been upholders of a great American tradition.

THE NEW AND THE OLD: THE COLONIAL AMERICAS IN WORLD HISTORY

The joint history of the Americas is important because of the impact of the whole continent on the world. If we chart and map the spread of the influence of the Americas on the world, the gap between the United States and the rest does not seem quite as daunting as the raw statistics of wealth and power might suggest. Until very late in the nineteenth century, the cultural exchanges were pretty much all one way across the Atlantic, as the Americas made themselves in a European image; and conscious as we are of the might and magnetism of the United States today, I think we underestimate the contribution of the rest of the hemisphere to the rest of the planet over a longer period.

The period began as soon as regular links with the Old World were forged. The era of the revelation that America existed, the period of the opening of the maritime routes that joined the New World to the rest of the world—this was a dawn that it was very heaven to observe. Columbus was hailed as "a hero such as the ancients made gods of" and "an apostle" who had executed a peregrination "more divine than human." It was "the greatest event since the Incarnation," in the opinion of Cortés's secretary. Adam Smith regarded the crossing of the Atlantic, together with the opening up of the Indian Ocean, as potentially the most significant event in history. These were predictions rather than appraisals. But they came true. They were already coming true when they were made.

The transformed image of the world, which emerged from systematic exploration of the new continent, renewed confidence in human powers: Carlos Borja did not feel he knew what the world was like until he held a globe in his hands in 1566. To be able to grasp its dimensions, attain its extent, and even, by the early eighteenth century, descry its shape helped to stimulate the "scientific revolution"— the conviction that creation could be mastered by experience and contained, under heaven, no mysteries that God had occluded from human vision. The New World's horn of plenty spilled treasure into the *Wunderkammern* of Europe, the protoscientific collections in which knowledge of the world was gathered. The Americas were an immense laboratory of observation and experiment for participants in seventeenth- and eighteenth-century debates about the nature, origins, and diversity of life. Charles Marie de la Condamine went to Quito to measure the earth. Alexander von Humboldt crisscrossed Spanish America to get to know the cosmos. Ultimately, specimens observed in America, especially in the Galápagos and Tierra del Fuego, while Darwin was aboard the *Beagle,* made a major contribution to the theory of evolution.

Ironically, meanwhile, contact with America initiated changes of even greater significance, beyond human control. What the great historian Alfred Crosby has called "the Columbian exchange" reversed millions of years of evolution: the tendency for the biota of sundered continents to diverge. Now a convergent era began, as the plants, fauna, microbes, and human types of the New World and the Old World invaded each other's territories, borne on the ships that carried explorers and adventurers, conquerors and missionaries, settlers and slaves. Nothing like it had been possible since Pangea shattered in fragments and the continents started to drift apart.

The convergence of biota accompanied a meeting of cultures. The human encounter between the peoples of the Old and New World had jarring effects on prevailing ideas about the nature of man. When Bartolomé de Las Casas (1484–1566) formulated, on the basis of his American experience, his view that "all the peoples of mankind are human," he was uttering not a platitude but a revolutionary summons to justice. From Pope Paul III's bull of 1533, endorsing human status for the natives of the New World, to Franz Boas's formulation of the doctrine of cultural relativism in the early twentieth century runs a long, thin line of continuity that leads to today's insistence on the universality of human rights and equality of treatment for all peoples, irrespective of color or culture.

Had they not lurked in the Americas, "noble savages" would surely have been found elsewhere; indeed, once located in America, they turned up, in effigy or simulacrum, in every clime and continent. Yet the New World has to be acknowledged as the place where the concept first took flesh. From the moment of Columbus's encounter with them—indeed, in contradictions already present in Columbus's mind as he first described them—pre-European inhabitants of the Americas evoked a divided response. To those who wanted to conquer, expropriate, and exploit them, they were brutish, uncivilizable, and irredeemable. To other beholders, who wanted to evangelize them, learn from them, or enjoy the benefits of collaboration with them, American natives—or some of them, at least—evinced positive qualities. Columbus cast them in a role he learned of from his Franciscan friends, as types of dependents on God in their nakedness and vulnerability—but he went on to slaughter and enslave as many as he could. Early humanist observers argued that the "Golden Age" of silvan innocence imagined by classical writers was embodied in native New World lives. Missionaries from the Catholic religious orders, striving to protect their flocks from secular depredations, catalogued natives' natural qualities: natural goodness, natural religion, natural sense of law and order.

Alternatively, alleged barbarism was excused as childlike unrestraint and therefore a sort of proof of innocence. For Montaigne, even the cannibals reported in Brazil had moral lessons for Europeans, who butchered one another with every conviction of self-righteousness and, with less sensibility than the cannibals', effectively "ate each other alive." Shakespeare's Caliban was poetically ambiguous—despised, subversive, sexually menacing, yet manifestly the victim of wrong.

These characterizations met in the type of the noble savage discovered in the seventeenth century by Jesuit missionaries among the Hurons. By comparison with their neighbors, the Hurons really did seem special. In particular, whereas other speakers of Iroquois languages identified the missionaries as enemies to be exterminated, the Huron saw them as potential friends, allies, and instructors in useful technologies. Missionary writings spread Huronophilia in Europe, with accounts full of Huron natural wisdom, mutual kindness, generosity to strangers, equality among themselves, love of peace, and strength in war. Their proficiency in arts and crafts—they were even credited with a rudimentary form of writing—contrasted with the wretchedness of savages who did not share the Hurons' native virtues.

Secular philosophers of the Enlightenment, who borrowed freely from Jesuit reports of the wider world, took up the ideal Huron with enthusiasm and adapted his message for their own purposes. The "ingenuous Huron" was the direct begetter of the noble savage; with wisdom uncorrupted by indoctrination, he became, in works by Lahontan, Voltaire, and Rousseau, the mouthpiece for criticism of church and state, the spokesman for liberty, equality, fraternity, and even free love. The socially inebriant potential of the image was distilled in a comedy of uncertain authorship, performed in Paris in 1768, that inspired or plagiarized Voltaire's portrait of a Huron sage. The Huron hero excels as lover, huntsman, and warrior while traversing the world with an intellectual's ambition—"to discover a little of how it is made." Love conquers reason when his inamorata is imprisoned in the Bastille; in a startling prefiguration of the liberation of 1789, he exhorts the mob to burn the roofs and breach the walls. The myth of the noble savage encouraged confidence in popular wisdom and therefore in popular sovereignty, the revolutionary battle cry of the late eighteenth century.

As well as changing the world's image, evolutionary trajectory, and revolutionary course, and the self-perception of humankind, the Americas also contributed to one of the most conspicuous economic transformations of modern history: a major shift in the world's economic balance. Until the treasure of the Americas became available to European exploiters, along with the new opportunities for wealth creation generated by an enormously expanded range of contacts, there was only one major axis of global trade: the silk roads and sea routes that linked Eurasia. Wealth was heavily concentrated at the eastern end of the axis, where the world's most industrialized and productive economies lay. Europe's appropriation of much of the Americas could not instantly end this ancient imbalance. Indeed, India maintained a favorable trading account with the West as a whole until the early nineteenth century. The disparity continued to favor China until the 1860s. But the inequalities started to diminish much earlier, from the late sixteenth century, when the output of the silver mines of

Peru and Mexico began to register an impact on the world economy. Westerners now had cash with which to invade Eastern marketplaces and capital to invest in new ways of wealth creation.

The process gathered momentum in the seventeenth and eighteenth centuries, as more of the Americas opened up, and as the new enterprises and products—the great plantations on the American coasts, the release of resources from the interior of the continent, the widening prospects of commerce—all contributed to the accumulation of capital in the Western world. Vital details of the story remain obscure or unresolved by fierce debate among historians. Did American specie drain eastward or enrich the West? What did slavery in the Americas contribute to industrialization in Europe? Was the economic ascent of the West a triumph of trade or a perquisite of power? Was the East bought out or ground down? The answers remain unknown, but the importance of the general context of the exploration and exploitation of America is beyond question. Put it this way: suppose Columbus had been right. Suppose the world was small and there was no room for America. Western Europe would have remained a small, backward region of Eurasia, dependent on the East for transfusions of technology, transmissions of culture, and transfers of wealth.

All these effects on world history, which have made the period since Columbus's voyages so different from that which preceded them, were collective achievements of the Americas. Their effect was already registered before the emergence of the United States. The States had a particular but not an exclusive role in the final arena of the Americas' impact on the world: the arena of new ideas. Romanticism was a European-born movement, but its nature and forms of expression owed part of their essence to

America. The scientists who accompanied Condamine's expedition to Quito in the 1730s, to measure variations in the sphericity of the earth, sent home extraordinary drawings—of volcanic eruptions, for instance, and arc lights in the sky—combining diagrammatic rigor with rugged romance. Cotopaxi became a romantic icon: the spiritual mountain home of the *Blaue Blüme*. American landscapes, from the Hudson Valley to the high Andes, reflected the romantic values with which painters beheld them in the nineteenth century. (Argentina was exceptional; there painters stuck to *costumbrismo*—genre painting in praise of the gauchos—and to visions of their country dominated by its people, not its landscapes. This probably reflects the collective neurosis of the beleaguered city dwellers about the contiguity of savagery, in an era when Argentina was an estuary and the pampa a palatinate. Elsewhere in the hemisphere, romantic sensibilities could be safely indulged.) The political counterparts of romanticism—modern republicanism, with its idealization of "the people," and socialism, practiced in backwoods utopias in early-nineteenth-century America—were tried out in the New World before they spread to the Old.

THE OLD AND THE NEW: HOW THE COLONIAL EXPERIENCE DREW THE AMERICAS TOGETHER

Of course, contact with the Old World transformed the New in ways that, if not uniform, were similar throughout the Americas. The effect generally was to meld the hemisphere—to unite its parts in common disasters, opportunities, and renewals. Demographic disaster hit almost everywhere the white man trod; guns, germs, and genocide combined to reduce the indigenous populations by perhaps 90 percent (the total figures are furiously disputed among historical demographers, but the proportion lost is widely agreed).

In most Spanish-ruled areas, where the Crown had a strong economic incentive to keep its native subjects alive and active, and where humane clergy wielded some power over the state, the recovery began early—around the end of the sixteenth century in some areas and during the eighteenth in most. This should not be mistaken as evidence that Spanish colonists were morally superior to others. In most of the regions they settled or ruled, they needed their Indians to supply labor and keep old, intensive agriculture going; they therefore strove to keep natives alive and bitterly regretted the visitations of plague that killed off their workers and tributaries. Spaniards blamed Indians for dying too easily. In areas where the natives were more of a hindrance than a help, Spanish authorities often broke their own rules of stewardship. In early-seventeenth-century Chile, Governor García Ramón frankly proclaimed a war of annihilation against the Mapuche; the effort was aborted not only because the clergy opposed it but also because it did not work.

For many peoples, by the time the demographic recovery started, it was already too late; in most of the Antilles, the indigenous people had already been exterminated and their culture had disappeared. In any case, slaughter of "Indians" resumed after independence in some formerly Spanish republics; systematic extermination, which had been unknown in colonial times, was introduced to southern Argentina by General Roca in the 1880s. Though not explicitly genocidal, a ruthless policy of total war transformed southern Chile, on the other side of the Andes, at about the same time, though only after a mad French squire from Dordogne tried to conquer Araucania, first for France, then as a private kingdom for himself, on the grounds that the natives were entitled to self-determination and that Chile had "no rights and her laws are ineffectual."

The apparently indomitable Mapuche had maintained an independent state—to the great admiration of romantics and liberals—throughout the colonial era. When Chile rebelled against Spain, the Mapuche discovered a previously undetected loyalty to the Spanish crown. The weak new republic was powerless to enforce its rule in Araucania, the unconquered Indian realm between the Bío-Bío and the Valdivia region. During the third quarter of the nineteenth century, however, Chile acquired the means and motive for a showdown. A worldwide population explosion boosted demand for Chilean nitrates and copper and generated the cash with which to buy "tools of empire"—steel cannon and Gatlings. Railways ripped into virgin territories. Settlers—growing in numbers as they spilled out of overpopulated Europe—renewed pressure on Indian lands. War broke out at the end of the 1860s. For much of the next decade, the Chilean effort was hampered by war on other fronts, against Peru and Bolivia. The Indians achieved a series of impressive defensive victories, comparable with the last-gasp victories of other victims of imperialism in the same period elsewhere in the world: the long-successful indigenous resistance during the Maori wars; the Sioux and Cheyenne triumph at Little Bighorn; the Zulu achievement at Isandhlwana. But, like all those victories, the Mapuches' were of short-lived effect. The Chilean strategy of penning their adversaries beyond fortified frontiers gradually pushed them into an unsustainable patch of territory. By 1883, they were beaten and confined to a small reservation within their former lands. They were still better off than their counterparts in Argentina or North America— who were exterminated or subjected to demoralizing forced migrations.

In areas of predominantly British colonization or "Anglo" rule, preconquest levels of demographic buoyancy have never really returned, outside the formerly Spanish southwest of the United States. The English colonies relied on imported labor—indentured or enslaved—and so could afford to massacre their Indians or drive them westward. They had a ready-made ideology of extermination. They were the new Israel. The Indians were the "uncircumcised," to be dealt with as old Israel dealt with Moab, Edom, and Philistia—smitten hip and thigh. The English, indifferent to clerical discipline, rarely endured Spanish-style agonies of conscience about the justice of their presence in America or the morality of their wars. People who left their land underexploited or unenclosed deserved to lose it. True tenure was proved only by the line of the fence or the marks of the plow. Indians in British areas of expansion were too poor to be worth exploiting for tribute. It was more economical to dispossess them and replace them with white farmers or black slaves. The only colony where this reasoning was modified was early Pennsylvania. Here, moral and material considerations combined to favor a policy of friendly collaboration with the Indians. Thanks to the founder's Quaker high morality, supposedly just prices were paid for land purchases from the natives, who were encouraged to stay on the frontier as buffers against hostile tribes or rival European empires. This equilibrium of "love and consent," however, was doomed to collapse in the eighteenth century as the pressure of white population grew and overspilled the limits of the state the founder had conceived.

Throughout British America, the native peoples were a source of conflict between frontiersmen and the representatives of the Crown, who wanted the protection of Indian buffer states and the benefit of a relatively dense pool of white labor, which frontier conquests would disperse. From the point of view of most colonial subjects, however, the Indians were mere impediments to landgrabbing. Genocide was the best means of dealing with them. In 1637 an explicit attempt to exterminate an entire people—the New England Pequot—was half finished in a massacre on Mystic River, where, the governor reported, the victims could be seen "frying in the fire and the streams of blood quenching the same." The tribe's very name was proscribed. In defiance of official policy, a settler malcontent, Nathaniel Bacon, launched war in Virginia in 1675 with the explicit aim of destroying all Indians, friendly and hostile alike. This was a characteristic outrage in the late seventeenth century, a period of increasing tension—which also provoked violent clashes in Spanish-settled areas in Florida and New Mexico—between growing colonies and threatened natives. In terms of the sacrifice of life on both sides, the worst such episode was King Philip's War in New England in 1675–1676. Launched by an Algonquin chief, who managed to put together an uncharacteristically big Indian coalition in an attempt to stem white expansion, this resistance movement threatened to reverse the direction of extermination; the white presence was, for a few months, genuinely in peril, until quisling tribes from the interior were drafted in on the colonists' side to restore the balance in the white man's favor.

Representatives of the British Crown made new attempts to modify frontier policy in favor of the Indians in the eighteenth century, when competition with the French empire increased the value of native friendship and compliance. Every victory against the French, however, and every accession of security, increased friction on Indian frontiers and sometimes prompted violent countermeasures by the colonial authorities and massacres of Indians by unruly colonists. Genocide resumed in the independent United States until the 1890s, when the last worthwhile Indian lands were stolen, the frontier was officially "closed," and the dead of Wounded Knee were buried. When the United States finally got around to counting its Indians in 1910, there were 266,000; at the best estimates, this was probably less than 10 percent of the population of the same area in the sixteenth century.

Similar practices were characteristic for even longer in Brazil. There the plight of the natives was exacerbated in the colonial era by laws that allowed them to be enslaved— three million, according to a contemporary estimate, on the Rio Negro alone in the hundred years up to 1750. Thirty-five percent of Brazilian native communities enumerated in 1900 had disappeared by about 1960. Callous expulsions, destructive expropriations, and informal massacres went on until the 1980s. During that decade, the great economist Walt Rostow was a visiting fellow at my college in Oxford. He used to tire me at dinner with assertions of the superior humanity, owed to the Portuguese tradition, of Brazilians over other Latin Americans. Eventually my patience snapped. "Forgive me," I said, "but don't

Brazilians massacre their Indians?" "Well," he replied, paus-ing to masticate a mouthful of *veau à la crème*, "they mas-sacre a few." Every multiculturalism has its limits, and Brazil, one of the world's first exemplary pluralist democ-racies, long made an exception of its Indians.

The demographic disaster helped spread around the hemisphere new economic practices: ranching, slave plan-tations, mining, wage labor, long-range trade. Ranching was a powerful new presence because it could transform the ecologies of vast regions and because the Americas offered so much propitious terrain. The Old World heartlands from which it was transposed were tiny by comparison—marginal cattle-rearing lands in Extremadura and shep-herders' narrow routes of transhumance, which crossed Castile. In the New World, ranching came to fill huge tracts of prairie, pampa, and sertão. Before the inruptions of Eu-ropean colonialism it was an almost unknown way of life. Although aquatic life-forms were farmed in many parts of the precolonial hemisphere, there were few land animals suitable for herding: only the llamas and vicuñas of the Andes were managed in this way and even then on a rela-tively small and restricted scale. For the development of herding for food, marginal land, unsuitable for human food crops, is essential; beyond the punas—the high grasslands—of the Andes, there were few places where this kind of en-vironment hosted an exploitable, domesticable species. The bighorn, as already mentioned, might have provided a useful case in North America, but its normal habitat seems to have been too high and cold for any but seasonal occu-pancy by the peoples who lived in the regions concerned. In other areas, native deer, bison, caribou, musk ox, and guanacos were at hand—but nowhere in proximity to peo-ples with the means or motives to domesticate them.

While ranching was made possible by new breeds of cattle from Europe, new European technologies transformed mining. The localized exploitation of placer metals and shallow mines yielded to large-scale extraction from deep mines and from ores that required high smelting temperatures or previously unavailable materials for amalgamation. As with ranching, the opportunities were on a new scale by comparison with the Old World. In the sixteenth century the Americas became a theater of seekers after "El Dorado"—fabulous gold-rich kingdoms of the kind Cartier sought along the Saint Lawrence, Coronado in Kansas, Raleigh in Guyana. As the myth of El Dorado, and others like it, forfeited confidence, real riches washed from the rivers or were revealed in the earth: in the sixteenth century the "silver mountains" of Zacatecas and Potosí and the emeralds of Esmeraldas; in the seventeenth and eighteenth, the gold and diamonds of Minas Gerais; in the nineteenth, the goals of the Californian and Alaskan gold rushes; and in between these spectacular cases, innumerable local gold rushes. Mining provided the means and the foci for the development of wage economies. Eventually, wages replaced systems of tribute, service, slavery, and subsistence farming, which provided labor for the pre-European economies. Eventually, instead of a world in which every society had its own system, the hemisphere became, more or less consistently, home to uniform capitalism.

Long-range trade, on a scale unimaginable before the European conquests, expanded the area of cultural exchange to embrace the whole hemisphere. It is not generally realized that in the colonial New World precolonial patterns of exchange often remained intact; European merchants joined existing trading communities, extending the reach or increasing the volume of traffic, enhancing what Indian Ocean venturers called "country trades," which involved local or regional exchanges that never touched Europe. In colonial North America, trade in deerskins and beaver pelts extended precolonial practice. The *coureurs des bois* and buckskin-clad frontiersmen slotted into an existing framework, which linked hunting grounds and routes of trade and tribute. The Huron, farmers and traders who did not need to hunt except as means of traditional exercise and dietary supplement, were the middlemen of the early-seventeenth-century fur trade, supplying French buyers in Québec. During the 1620s they supplied ten to twelve thousand pelts a year. A few years ago I stumbled across a fascinating document, now over four hundred years old, from colonial Venezuela. It had ended up in—of all places—the Public Record Office in London, where, presumably, it had arrived via an English pirate ship, which must have captured the mail vessel in which, in about 1594, the document was bound for Spain. It explains how Spanish entrepreneurs took part in a profitable canoe-borne trade in local textiles, natural pharmaceuticals, and dyestuffs along the coast of Venezuela in the 1590s. Similarly, the economy that sustained the conquerors of Yucatán was no trans-oceanic affair of precious goods but an extension of the age-old trade with central Mexico, based largely on cacao for consumption in Mexico City.

Of course, Spanish activity was not confined to modest ventures of these kinds, along traditional grooves. The Spanish monarchy was a great inaugurator of new intra-American trade routes. New cities, founded in places never settled on a large scale before, especially on the Pacific and Atlantic coasts, became magnets for the supply of foodstuffs, cotton textiles, and building materials. The conquest of Peru from 1527 to 1533 demanded a new transcontinental route across the Isthmus of Panama, which became, like the alternative later opened from Bolivia to the Atlantic via the River Plate, a major silver-bearing artery of the Spanish empire. The new mining ventures in remote hinterlands were served by mule-train routes, which the indigenous civilizations had never required. The conquest of much of Chile in the mid–sixteenth century stimulated the creation of a heroic new seaborne route, far into the Pacific, to overcome the Humboldt Current; it took longer for sailing ships to get from Lima to Concepción than from Seville to Santo Domingo.

The slow but inexorable spread of Spanish frontiers brought regions formerly unknown to one another into touch; the link between Mexico and Peru is the most startling case, since it seems incredible—yet true—that the civilizations of those areas never had any significant mutual contact until the Spaniards arrived. Although the places Spaniards occupied in New Mexico, Arizona, and Texas had shown some signs of Mexican cultural influences in the past, California was a genuinely new discovery, where Spanish missions in the eighteenth century created for the first time ventures in settlement and agriculture that made the region a potential trading partner for other parts of the monarchy. It would have been possible for indigenous merchants to navigate the Amazon and the Orinoco before the coming of the Spaniards, but as far as we know, they never did so. Those mighty and mysterious waterways were not fully exploited as arteries of commerce until well into the seventeenth century, after the efforts of such heroic explorers as Pedro Teixeira, who in 1639 demonstrated that the Amazon could be navigated upriver from the Atlantic to the vicinity of Quito, or Miguel de Ochogavia, "the Columbus of the Apure," who in 1647 celebrated his own achievement in doggerel:

> I came, I saw, I conquered, and returned in glory
> From Orinoco—crystals cleft and fears allayed.
>
> To God I dedicate, in thanks, my wondrous story,
> To you, my readers, all the benefits to trade.

Historians of the new commerce opened up by the Spanish empire have traditionally concentrated on the world-changing transoceanic trades: the *carrera de Indias,* which linked Spain to America and injected Europe's specie-starved economies with veins of bullion; the slave suppliers' *asientos,* which let other European merchants into the Spanish main and linked the Americas to Africa; and the route of the Manila galleon, which made an annual crossing of the Pacific to Acapulco, facilitating the direct exchange of Mexican silver for Chinese manufactures. But from the point of view of American history, the new intra-American ventures were more important; the routes laced together formerly sundered parts of the hemisphere, making it possible to think of an ever-bigger area as a whole. In North America the fur traders—though Eurasian markets were overwhelmingly the ultimate destination of their wares—were also developers of "country trades," gradually pushing their supply routes further into the interior. Toward the end of the colonial period it was the development of the Mississippi-Missouri river system as a new highway of trade that made the Louisiana question so vital and led to the bewildering turnover in sovereignty claims, until they were resolved in favor of the United States in 1803.

Trade's tendency to mesh ever-growing parts of the Americas together accelerated in the postcolonial period. Richard Henry Dana's famous experience of his *Two Years Before the Mast* (1840) illustrates the remarkable initiative that linked California and New England by sea. After a voyage around the continent via Cape Horn—a notoriously backbreaking route that compelled sailors to strain at the yards, hauling to beat the wind—they stretched hides on the beach near Los Angeles and attended the wedding of a Yankee businessman, tight-lipped and stovepipe-hatted, to a beguiling señorita; this was how California began to be linked, culturally and commercially, into the life of the United States before the continent could be safely or reliably crossed by land. The meshing and melding of the Americas continued with the pioneers—explorers, scientists, trappers, Jesuits, Mormons, and miners—who painfully picked out transcontinental and interriver routes in the early nineteenth century. The wagon trains and railway surveyors followed.

Where trade routes grow, transfers of biota follow. The ecological exchanges that accompanied and followed colonialism happened across the Americas as well as across the oceans. Today the same varieties of maize are grown in North Dakota as in Mexico and Argentina. Turkeys, unknown outside Mesoamerica at the time of the conquest, have become the Thanksgiving Day dish of the United States. Chiles have conquered northern palates. The defining ingredients of Mexican cuisine stake out ever more of the culinary territory. Chili is the hot brand of this cuisine, corn and black beans its solid symbols; limes provide its lashings; filmy expanses of cheese form its flag. Chili con carne is its signature dish. Chili is part of the story of the Americanization of America, made from the repertoire of ingredients that predated the American annexation of the Southwest and that, since then, have gradually conquered the conquerors.

The menu of ecological exchange includes peanuts, which originated in Peru, where they were grown by the beginning of the third millennium B.C. They almost certainly reached North America by a circuitous route—first taken by the Portuguese to western Africa, then carried back to the New World as food on slave ships. Early in the second half of the nineteenth century a black American agronomist, George Washington Carver, appreciated their potential as an answer to one of the world's great shortages: lack of fat, which had become scarce owing to a huge increase in demand from the world's growing population and the burgeoning munitions industry, which needed new means of greasing cartridges. He developed ways of milling them for their high oil content as well as for exploiting the whole nuts for food. Today the United States is the world's third-biggest producer, after China and India. The state of Georgia dominates the industry in a country where peanut butter is a comforting delicacy, associated with the security of childhood and mother love. Jimmy Carter's role as a peanut farmer helped his image of folksy reliability during his presidential election campaign in 1976, when TV commercials showed him running his crop through his hands. Tomatoes, which were of Andean origin and were important in the cuisine of ancient Mesoamerica, also had to be introduced to North America via the Old World; they arrived only in the eighteenth century. Yet, thanks in large part to the popularity of tomato ketchup as a relish for hot

dogs and hamburgers, they are now the second most important vegetable, by volume consumed, in the United
States. Only potatoes exceed them; and these are another
South American cultivar—one of the oldest in the world,
originating from an Andean tuber and first cultivated perhaps as much as ten thousand years ago—that relied on
European agents to carry it to North America.

THE COLONIAL BALANCE

On the whole, the effect of the colonial experience was
to make the Americas more like each other, not to drive
them apart. Colonialism introduced a layer of political
authority—the rule of strangers—that was similar wherever it was established; never before in recorded history
had there been anything like such a uniform political order
over so much of the Americas. It brought a common
religion—for Christianity, whether in the Protestant or
Catholic tradition, was remarkably uniform compared with
the paganism that had preceded it. The European intruders spread consistent technologies for making wealth and
making war. They introduced common economic practices, a common system of writing, uniform conventions and
rituals of public life, consistent notions of the meaning of
childhood and marriage, kinship and consanguinity, friendship and enmity, war and peace, love and death. None of
these things had ever been uniform, as far as we know,
across the Americas before. So, toward the end of the colonial era, the common features of history in the Americas
were still conspicuous—more conspicuous, indeed, in important respects, than the differences.

Spanish colonies formed a vast new framework for cultural exchange. In the first two centuries of the Spanish

presence there was abundant material evidence of the outward spread of culture from the historic heartlands of the Americas. Jesuit churches appeared in Amazonia and the Chaco. Spanish cities sprang up deep in the South American cone, which had never known urban civilization before. In the eighteenth century, Franciscan missions and military presidios crept along the California coast and into the desert frontier with the North American prairie, while Spanish agents negotiated the submission of native peoples as far north as the Mandan of the upper Missouri and south as far as the Huiliches beyond the Bío-Bío. Castilian became an enduring lingua franca over most of the hemisphere. By comparison, Anglo-America was a modest and precarious affair. Before the nineteenth century its territorial gains at Spanish expense were meager: Jamaica and a few more Caribbean islands and, latterly, Florida. When and how did the balance of power and potential shift in the Anglos' favor? And why and how did the great nineteenth-century divergence come about, launching North America, and the United States in particular, on a hectic course toward domination not only of the hemisphere but also, eventually, of the world? Common sense directs inquiry toward the turbulent era of transition in which the colonial period came to an end.

THE
INDEPENDENCE
ERA

THE LANDWARD TURN

In the eighteenth century, the shape and nature of European imperialism in the Americas were transformed by what I call the landward turn: the enterprise of opening up the continental interiors. In the Spanish colonies, this process had begun long before on a fairly large scale. In those of Britain, France, and Portugal, only very tentative beginnings had been registered earlier. In the eighteenth century things evened out.

Until then, North America proved relatively hard to populate. Sixteenth-century attempts to found North American colonies almost all failed. Those founded in the seventeenth century took a long time to make the breakthrough into viability—renewing their populations, that is, by sustainable birthrates. They could not rely, as most of Spain's early American conquests could, on native population levels to keep them viable. Although there are no estimates of the size of the indigenous population of North America at contact time—credible, well-informed guesses range from two to four million—there is no doubt that the northern moiety of the hemisphere was sparsely populated. And such people as it did have were not well suited, by sedentary vocation, to be a labor force for colonial empires, such as the big, densely packed native populations of Mesoamerica and the Andes provided for Spain.

Immigration could not, at first, make up the deficit. Most migrants to Virginia died without surviving issue, until the second half of the seventeenth century, and life expectancy remained low. Few colonists saw the better side

of fifty. The Virginia swampland, where the first permanent settlements were founded from 1607 onward, was so
unhealthy that of the first hundred or so settlers, only
thirty-eight were still alive nine months after landing. Of
the first three thousand, only a couple of hundred were
still alive after a bloody war with the natives in 1622. The
population did not begin to increase naturally until some
fifty years after the first settlement. The breakthrough was
accompanied by increased rates of immigration, which
tripled in the period from about 1650 to 1670.

New England's environment was less hostile: "endowed
with grace and furnished with means," as a Puritan settler
declared. From early in the 1630s the colonists could grow
enough to feed themselves, and natural increase kept the
population growing. Without valuable cash products, however, the region was of little appeal to immigrants: only
twenty-one thousand came in the whole seventeenth century, and the numbers diminished, with only a third of that
total arriving after 1640. These were problems general to
northern colonies. There were only five thousand people
in New Netherland when the colony collapsed in 1664.
New France received fewer than four thousand immigrants
in the second half of the seventeenth century. France,
though densely populated by European standards in early
times, was never able to extrude many colonists.

In consequence, the French were unable to imitate the
Spanish and Portuguese by creating great land empires in
the American interior. The British began to do so only in
the late eighteenth century, when immigration soared and
settlers from New England overspilled into the Ohio region. These are important facts, because in the long run
the test by which the success of American colonization has
been judged has been action in the continental interior;

this is the direction in which "the course of empire takes its way." Colonies that clung to the coasts could never be fully American—rather, they tended to remain outposts of Europe or edges of oceanic civilizations.

European maritime empires were bound, sooner or later, to lumber onto land, where traditional imperialism led. For the difference between a sea empire and a land empire is more than a mere matter of location or of geographical characterization or classification. Sea empires are empires of trade, which they seek always to channel and sometimes to control. Land empires attempt additionally or instead to control production. Columbus envisaged a trading setup when he first encountered Hispaniola, imagining a European merchant colony under a Castilian aegis, trading in cotton, mastic, and slaves. Really, none of these products were available in large quantities. Instead, economic policy became riveted on the gold mines of the island. Columbus's war of conquest of 1495–1496 can be represented, albeit on a small scale, as the first step toward the creation of the Spanish territorial empire.

The conquest of Mexico marked a breakthrough into a new kind of imperialism: the acquisition of vast inland territories. The conquests of the 1530s and 1540s in Peru and Colombia were also essentially of highland empires, while the acquisition of Paraguay took Spaniards far upriver into the depths of the continent. By the midcentury the Spanish empire was no longer merely a "seaborne," much less a "seaboard," affair, such as most other European states would found, but drew vital resources of tribute and silver from deep inland. In 1598 the conquerors of New Mexico, in their ignorance of North American geography, hoped they were acquiring a province with easy access to the Pacific; in reality, they added another landbound zone to the monarchy. Meanwhile, religious orders, especially the Jesuits in midmost South America, began to open up another vast land empire, with a large native population, for Spain.

Other European empires in the Americas, without the advantage of exploitable local labor sources on the scale of the Spanish lands, tended at first to expand to landward on only a very modest scale; they stuck near the coasts to increase the areas where they could cultivate the crops they introduced, such as sugar in the Caribbean, tobacco in Virginia, rice in the Carolinas, and wheat almost everywhere. Sometimes spectacular effects could be achieved in a small space: France's colony of Saint-Domingue in the eighteenth century occupied only half the island of Hispaniola—hardly much of a land empire in terms of size, but an island of *Wirtschaftswunder,* which became, for a while, the world's major producer of coffee and sugar. The local product of Brazil that first attracted commercial attention on a fairly large scale was logwood. Sugar soon replaced it, but it was a laborious crop to plant, harvest, and refine, greedy of capital and demanding lots of specialized labor. It was suitable only to coastal enclaves, where it could be successfully grown and from which it could be easily shipped, and it would never, on its own, have induced planters to create a large territorial domain in Brazil's hinterland.

Portugal's early interest in the interior of Brazil was of a similar character, provoked by Spanish interest in the navigation of the Amazon in the early seventeenth century. Portuguese attention, however, became increasingly focused on Brazil as the century wore on and the empire was restructured. Strained by long wars with the Netherlands and Spain—more significantly, pressurized and overawed by the rise of such dauntingly powerful indigenous Asian states as those of the Mughals, the Tokugawa shoguns, and the Safavids in the time of Shah Abbas—Portugal withdrew from most of her sovereign outposts in the East. Brazil became, *faute de mieux*, the jewel in the crown of a now compact empire. Most of the Brazilian coast was less than two months' sail from Lisbon or the African slave ports. Even so, the state was slow to undertake the risks and costs of landward imperialism. The hinterland empire remained largely an affair of private slavers and ranchers until the 1680s, when reports of gold and diamond finds deep in the interior began to accumulate. By early in the second half of the century, aggressive activity had pushed Spanish outposts back roughly to the line of the present linguistic boundary. Although Spain's New World land empire was much greater in extent, Portugal's was in some ways more extraordinary, carved out of hostile environments, where there was little useful manpower and where most of what manpower there was had to be caught, enslaved, and forcibly redistributed.

By then the landward temptation had seduced Britain and France into attempts to imitate Spain's New World mainland empire. Britain's American land empire wore a substantial look because of its large immigrant population and the enthusiasm with which, from the 1760s, settlers moved to open up the interior. France's in Louisiana was little more than an outline on the map; Frenchmen, despite the density of their home population, were reluctant emigrants in the eighteenth century. Still, both states claimed, if they did not effectively exercise, control of great swathes of the North American hinterland prior to French withdrawal in 1763. In part, these were preemptive and speculative ventures, designed to exclude Spain from areas of as yet largely unknown potential. The landward turn, which focused vision on the continental interiors, wrenched the attention of colonial elites away from Europe toward potential new empires of their own.

A further consequence was that Britain had a brand-new empire, in which a brand-new society suddenly took shape in the third quarter of the eighteenth century. As the colonial horizon broadened, immigration exploded. An astonishing population increase—to nearly two and a half million, by a factor of ten within three generations—filled a burgeoning world and an expanding frontier. Between the middle of the eighteenth century and the outbreak of the American Revolution, the populations of Georgia and South Carolina trebled; that of Virginia doubled. From about 1760 a rush of settlers scaled the Appalachians to their "new Canaan" between the Ohio and the Susquehanna, reoccupying the territory of America's earliest-known inhabitants (see page 26). Michel-Guillaume de Crèvecoeur, who was to become the first anatomizer of independent American identity when he wrote "What Is an American?," imagined himself joining the mass of immigrants heading into the wilds of Pennsylvania and "a prodigious number of houses rearing up, fields cultivating, that great extent of industry opened up to a bold and indefatigable people." When the land office opened at Fort Pitt in 1769, it registered 2,790 claims on the first day. Ten thousand families lived on this frontier by 1771. Many of the "hearts and minds" in which the Revolution was conceived were those of newcomers, gripped in a ferment of exciting possibilities. British America was a colony in flux, exploding with instability. Independent America was, to a great extent, a nation of latecomers.

New England, meanwhile, resembled, without conscious imitation, the remoter Spanish colonies in under-populated zones, such as sub-Araucanian Chile or the

River Plate region. Slaves were unsuited to the climate and unaffordable to the economy. New England was launched by a form of danegeld: subsidies and supplies extorted from the natives by the threat of war. It was saved from early extinction by its maritime outlook. Farmer-settlers worked wonders with rocky soils—which were duly abandoned, to be replaced by mills or returned to forest, as newer, better farmland opened up farther west. But New Englanders could never fully participate in the landward turn. Mountain barriers and the boundaries of rival states cut their maritime colonies off from the interior. They were best equipped for a seaborne venturers' economy. The impoverished hinterland drove work and wealth creation seaward, to the cod and whale fisheries and long-range trade. In a sense, this was the wages of success; early in the eighteenth century, New England's population outgrew the colonies' capacity to grow food. A trading vocation replaced the farming vocation with which the founding fathers had arrived.

Yet New Englanders in their own way, by sea, drifted apart from the "mother country," England, just as the landward-driving settlers and investors in the Ohio edged away by land. For the ocean led to the world. Ever-improving maritime technology was always—slowly, by little, incremental advances or by sudden leaps, such as the introduction of longitude-finding means in the late eighteenth century—opening more of the globe to commerce. Gradually, in the course of the century, it became a marked disadvantage for a trading people to be constrained by empire. New England's quarrels with Britain focused increasingly on issues of untrammeled trade and the freedom of the seas, and disputes over the definition of contraband. The great symbolic acts of resistance that preceded the Revolutionary War were offshore "incidents" that made these issues explicit in acts of civil disobedience: the Boston Tea Party in 1774 and the seizure of the *Gaspée* in Providence Harbor in 1772. "God damn your blood!" screamed the respectable merchants who boarded and burned this piracy-control vessel.

THE STATE OF THE ARTS

According to some Latin Americans, the arts are the one area of civilized achievement in which they have never yielded their former supremacy to the Yankees. In the seventeenth century and for most of the eighteenth it was easy for the old centers of civilization to maintain their output of art under Spanish management. Anglo-America had none of the advantages of tradition, momentum, and wealth on which that output relied. It lacked courtly life; the viceroy of New Spain maintained a studio of "Aztec painters" in the 1540s. The poetry of Sor Juana de la Cruz, the preeminent colonial-period writer anywhere in the New World, was supported by the viceroys of her day. Universities were founded and printing presses imported in Mexico and Peru within a few years of the conquistadores' arrival. In the second half of the seventeenth century, when the domestic Spanish economy underwent agonizing contractions preceding a modest new birth, Mexico and Peru provided markets for the otherwise unsalable works of genius of the Sevillan school. Transpacific contacts that brought examples of the arts of the Orient, and especially of China and the Philippines, to the Spanish colonies further enriched the heritage.

It would be unfair, however, to compare the arts of the fledgling English colonies with those of the relatively old and immeasurably richer settlements of Spain. A better comparison can be made with Brazil. Before the nineteenth century, the most impressive extensions of civilization into new areas occurred in the southern parts of the continent and Brazil was the location of the most conspicuous instance. In 1500, Pedro Alvares Cabral dedicated the land to the Holy Cross. Brazil seemed blessed. The first Jesuits in this, the Company's earliest overseas mission field, found the footprints of Saint Thomas in Bahía. Yet for almost the first two centuries of colonialism, there was little money for art. Colonial penetration was superficial and the sources of wealth were few: logging at first, then the coast-hugging sugar industry. The hinterlands of the Portuguese and short-lived Dutch colonies were left to the Indians and their persecutors, the slavers of São Paulo. Indigenous arts featherwork, mask making, body painting—were unappreciated by the colonists, but even in this period the country wrought a small revolution in art history, thanks to the illustrators and engravers of flora and wildlife and native life, who introduced European artists to a new repertoire of images and an unprecedented vision of lushness and savagery.

The size and wealth of the country grew gradually in the seventeenth century. Politics and commerce opened the hinterland, first in response to Spanish forays along the Amazon, then as Dutch and native competitors drove the Portuguese empire out of most of its Asian stations. The process became an explosion in the "golden century" from the 1690s, when gold and diamonds replaced sugar as Brazil's "monoculture." An era of ambitious demand for high art began in a land awash with wealth. Some cash went on British services and manufacturers, stimulating "the first industrial revolution." Some of it ended up in India and China, funding the Western world's abiding balance-of-payments deficit with the East. Much of it gilded altars and funded the creativity of sculptors and painters. Gold and silverwork were banned in 1766 to protect Portuguese craftsmen, but a native tradition had already been established—by indigenous craftsmen, trained by Franciscans and Jesuits, such as made an altarpiece in Grao Para reputedly "equal to any in Lisbon," and, above all, by mulattos and blacks.

By universal acclaim, the greatest of them was the mulatto cripple Aleijadinho, born in about 1732, the illegitimate son of a Portuguese carpenter and his slave. After a supposedly wild youth, which may be a pious fiction, he was divinely chastised with leprosy, muscular dystrophy, partial paralysis, and the loss of his toes. He carved masterpieces outside churches in Minas Gerais, with a chisel tied to half-paralyzed fingers. His embittered, contorted style climaxed in his last sculptures, a series of twelve prophets at Congonhas do Campo. The animation, emotion, and decorative detail would have been impossible for the sculptor's crippled hands but for the local soapstone, which is soft when freshly quarried and hardens on exposure to air.

What Aleijadinho was to sculpture, the slave boy Manuel da Cunha was to painting. Born in Rio in 1737, he was sent to Lisbon for his natural talent to be trained, then returned to decorate Rio churches with scenes animated by pathos: the miracles of Saint Francis, the descent from the cross. He did many secular portraits, becoming the first black, the first Brazilian, to excel in the field.

Yet as the generation of Cunha and Aleijadinho grew old, the balance of excellence in the arts was beginning to shift, or to grow more even, between the Latin and Anglo moieties of the Americas. The third quarter of the eighteenth century was a period of astonishingly rapid maturation in the arts of the English mainland colonies, especially in painting, silversmiths' work, and architecture. The early-eighteenth-century height of fashion was to build in wood and make it look like stone. No self-respecting mansion dweller of the second half of the century would build in such a modest material. A visitor to John Brown's "homestead" in Providence, Rhode Island, found it resembled "some noblemen's seats in England" and "surpasses any I have seen." George III got one of his best court painters, Benjamin West, from America. Jacques-Louis David is supposed to have asked why all the best English painters were Americans. The explanation is crudely economic: in the same period, the trade of the northern colonies and the slave-based productivity of the southern ones made Anglo-America one of the richest societies per capita in the world. The flowering of the arts was fertilized by the multiplication of patronage. After the colonial era, while the United States continued to get richer and import and create more arts, the former Spanish colonies seemed to stagnate. Eliza Lynch introduced the first piano to Asunción. Chile never heard the complete cycle of Beethoven symphonies until 1913.

TOWARD INDEPENDENCE

If the eighteenth century was a critical period in spreading uniform biota across the hemisphere and equalizing the state of the arts, it was no less important in the exchange of political ideas. Common notions—of popular sovereignty, of the virtues of republicanism and citizenship, of "the rights of man and of the citizen," of colonial dignity, and of the rule of written constitutions and codified laws—spread around the hemisphere. They became shared ideas in

Spanish and English colonies and the vocabulary of a common, pan-"American" discourse. They took flesh and blood in revolutionary wars of independence that between 1776 and 1829 "liberated" the United States and much of the rest of the American mainland—but not Canada or the Caribbean outside Haiti. Although the revolutions had very different results, the causes were similar: resentful local elites resisting the growing interference of intrusive governments from their "mother countries."

The aspirations of American revolutionaries were unoriginal. Demands for fiscal exemption would not have shocked a noble frondeur of the mid–seventeenth century. That institutions representative "of the people" should at least share sovereignty with the Crown was a principle of English Whigs and radical philosphes. The Minutemen on Lexington Green stood shoulder to shoulder with the shades of citizen armies idealized by Renaissance humanism. The language of rights and republics could be traced back to the writings of "commonwealthmen" in the English revolution, in the English colonies, and the *comunero* tradition in those of Spain, but both had remoter common origins in Renaissance civics and the inspiration of ancient Rome.

Throughout the hemisphere, revolutionary principles were promoted by readers of Rousseau, Machiavelli, and Tom Paine, and defended in part by soldiers of fortune recruited in Britain, Ireland, and Germany. The patriot fathers who employed these volunteers were, in some cases, so saturated in European precedents that they devised constitutions like the first Colombian republic's, described by the acclaimed founder of the nation as "a Greek temple on a Gothic pedestal." Intellectually, these were revolutions made in Europe. The official rhetoric of the revolutions was borrowed from Europe, and their leaders were pursuing Old World images of themselves.

This is an important point to acknowledge, because in one respect the impact of the Old World on the New in colonial times has been exaggerated. The prevailing notion, widely canvassed and fairly widely adopted by historians, is that in the early stages of the development of colonial government, where Europeans settled, colonialism eliminated the chieftainly model from America and replaced it with "feudal" practices, derived from Europe. It is true, of course, that some colonies of Europeans, where they existed, were administered by means familiar in Europe, by aristocratic paladins with daunting paper powers and only a remote Crown to restrain them: the *capitães generais* of Portuguese Brazil, the Spanish viceroys, the "Baronet of Nova Scotia," the lords proprietor of Delaware and Maryland, and all the other similarly arcane dignitaries who mediated European power in the Americas.

That was not, however, how white imperialism worked in most places, where the indigenous peoples continued to preponderate and where traditional ways of life continued from precolonial into colonial times. Here political relationships with the white man were affected by collaboration with incumbent elites, by the use of native allies and surrogates, or by what I call the "stranger effect"—by which I mean the way in which some peoples, because of cultural traits well represented in parts of the New World, responded with deference or submission to the stranger from afar; thus unarmed friars could dethrone idols in Mexico and yet command the communities they invaded; Jesuits could beguile Guaraní with no weapon more potent than music; Captain John Smith could, by his own account, win over the Powhatan with lessons in cosmology; Alvar

Núñez Cabeza de Vaca could establish renown as a holy man and acquire hundreds of Indian followers; even Cortés could march to Mexico with near impunity, indemnified by the benefit of Aztec doubts.

In partial consequence, the Americas really did form a "new world" of politics, where political institutions were new growths, resulting from interaction between natives and newcomers, not transplants from a European "home." The pioneering enterprise, moreover, threw up new political solutions to match new kinds of social effects, new microsocieties: the shipboard world of the migrants, the missions, the slave plantations, the maroon kingdoms, the commonwealths and companies of English "pilgrims," the *casas pobladas* of Spanish colonists with their curious ethnic mixtures and evolved notions of nobility. New social categories emerged: all the grades of *mestizaje*, black slavery on a large scale, the myriad varieties of indigenous dependency, the deference to wealth and godliness and intellect that became characteristic of some self-governing colonies.

A new political environment took shape. Historians have scoured sixteenth-century Europe for the origins of the "modern state," in which the feudal tier of devolved authority shrank to insignificance; the Crown enforced an effective monopoly of jurisdiction; the independence of towns withered; the Church submitted to royal control; and sovereignty—formerly definable on terms of jurisdiction—became increasingly identified with supreme legislative power, as statutes multiplied. No such state really existed in Europe, but some of the new political arrangements contrived in the Americas—especially in the Spanish American empire—achieved a close resemblance to it.

Here town councils were largely composed of royal nominees; ecclesiastical patronage was exclusively at the disposal of the Crown; with a few exceptions, feudal tenure was banned. There were Spaniards with rights, granted by the Crown or by royal representatives, in Indian labor services and tribute; typically, they practiced what I call fantasy feudalism, speaking of Indians as their vassals, but they were usually forbidden formal rights of jurisdiction and the "vassals" in question were really vassals only of the king. A stream of new legislation regulated—or, with varying degrees of effectiveness, was formulated to regulate—the new society. It might be exaggerated to call the Spanish empire in America an absolutism tempered by inefficiency or frustrated by distance, but it was a modern state, because it was a bureaucratic state and a statute state.

In the eighteenth century—and especially in its third quarter—the British empire in the New World came increasingly, in these respects, to resemble that of Spain. It got big by conquest, mainly at French expense, and expanded to landward. There it acquired new indigenous subjects. It exploded into wealth as a result of the great new global opportunities for commerce and the framework for trade that the British empire provided. It became relatively populous. Under the stress of war with France and in the flush of victory that ensued after the collapse of France's American empire in 1763, Britain's attitude toward America became more centralizing and interventionist. The British colonies had been what Richard Ford might have called "an unamalgamating bundle," all with their own institutions and "liberties" that impeded some of the most crucial functions of government, especially the billeting of troops and the exaction of taxes. An era of increasingly vigorous government from Britain was designed to make the administration more uniform, to exploit fiscally the colonies' growing wealth and security, and to organize defense on modern and efficient and, therefore, more centralized lines.

These measures incurred the resentment of conservative revolutionaries, anxious to retain the privileges and liberties that had accrued during the long period in which the home government had taken little interest in their affairs. The new demands of the prerevolutionary years came not so much from the colonists as from an England eager to exact efficiency from her empire. It was the threat to the colonies' comfortable habits of effective self-rule and cheap government that provoked confrontation. Washington and Jefferson were provincial English gentlemen only somewhat further removed from court than the leaders of country parties traditional in English politics.

A period of increasing interventionism from Europe and increasing friction with colonial elites was broadly paralleled in the Spanish monarchy, where "reformist" governments in the same period took increasingly burdensome measures in a similar spirit: reasserting bureaucratic controls, reorganizing imperial defense, eliminating traditional anomalies, maximizing the power and fiscal reach of the Crown. Spanish intendants were as intrusive and troublesome in Spanish colonies as governors were in those of Britain. In both empires, the home governments tried to ease local bigwigs out of influential offices and replace them with creatures of the metropolis. In both empires the results included growing, and potentially revolutionary, resentments. For both empires the Americas housed some of the remotest, most intractable provinces with the most marked peculiarities of interest. In both empires the home governments encouraged militarization—mobilization and training for defense. This was a rational response to the problems of security in vast territories with ill-defined frontiers, but the effect was to create potential reservoirs of armed revolutionaries.

The American revolutions—the convulsions of the period from 1776 to 1829, which separated most of the mainland European colonies from their "mother countries" and turned them into independent states—were in some ways, perhaps, stages in the divergence of the lands of the United States from those of the states that sprang up to her south. For the United States emerged from its Revolutionary War with a strength and potential for expansion far greater than those of any other country in the Americas. On the other hand, the revolutions can be seen as the last great common American experience.

In the 1770s the uprising in thirteen of the English mainland colonies used to be pictured as a peculiarly English affair—the inevitable outcome of long-standing traditions of freedom, which colonists had taken with them as a heritage from deep in the English past. On the contrary, current scholarship tells us, it was an extemporized solution to short-term problems, a typical convulsion of an Atlantic world that was full of rebellions in the late eighteenth century, from Socorro to Spithead and from Urubamba to Ulster. The Seven Years' War, which ended in 1763, created the necessary preconditions for the one feature that made the American Revolution exceptional: its success. By removing a French threat to the colonists' security, the war freed the colonies to challenge their rulers in England. The emergence of a buffer zone of Indian states in the hinterland created flash points of conflict between the empire, which needed to preserve the Indians, and the colonists, who wanted to exterminate them. By imposing high costs on imperial defense, the war encouraged Britain to seek new ways of taxing America, with all the familiar consequences. It trained American fighters in the skills they would need if they were ever to challenge British forces. The experience of military collaboration between American militias and British regulars initiated or exposed cultural incompatibilities: the brutalities of regular army discipline repelled the militias, while colonial resistance to billeting betokened, in army eyes, "neglect of humanity" and "depravity of nature." The colonists saw themselves as "trueborn Englishmen" but were disconcerted to find that their perception was not shared by their fellow countrymen across the Atlantic. The result was a history of mutual alienation that led to violence.

A "creole mentality"—a sense of a difference of interests and, perhaps, of nature—set the colonists apart from their metropolitan masters and partners and grew markedly in the decade preceding the Declaration of Independence. By "creole" I mean an identity espoused by colonials distinct from that of the mother country. In Spanish colonies, creole consciousness was precocious; in some ways it was evident in the first generation of the conquistadores. Pride in mixed ancestry—or false claims to it—was one sure sign. So was the use of indigenous languages alongside or instead of the metropolitan tongue. Fernando de Alva Ixtlilxochitl's (1578–1650) was a typically self-conscious native voice: a historian of his community in Texcoco, a Nahuatl interpreter in the courts, a government representative on several municipal councils, a promoter and compiler of collections of Nahuatl literature. In the same period, the royal Inca blood of Garcilaso de la Vega made him highly sought after as a godparent by young families in the Spanish town where he lived.

By the eighteenth century, creolism—it might fairly be said—was a strong Spanish-American ideology. The elite of Peru affected native dress and collected native artifacts. In Mexico, interest in native antiquities was boosted by discoveries in the late eighteenth century, including the "Maya Pompeii"—the ruins of Palenque—in 1773 and the uncovering of the Aztec "calendar stone" under the paving of the main square of Mexico City in 1790. The ruins of Xochicalco—the most complete survival from Aztec times—began to be systematically described at about the same time. Creole science responded to European savants' contempt for America by arguing that American nature was superior to that of the Old World—according to some claims, even the sky was more benign and astral influences more favorable. Indigenism served creolism but was not a necessary part of it. Creole sentiment could develop simply by way of colonial self-differentiation from both indigenous and metropolitan identities.

These movements in Hispanic America had parallels in the thirteen colonies. In Thomas Jefferson's mind, the right of trueborn Englishmen came to include the right to renounce English identity; Americans were founding a new society, independent of Britain, just as their Saxon forebears had founded a new society independent of Germany. This was the reason for his frustrated efforts to have Hengist and Horsa adorn the seal of the United States. At Jefferson's Monticello, his domestic museum was rich in American specimens and native artifacts. Painted buffalo hides hung in his hall. "Savage" carvings from Tennessee lined his atrium, rather as a Renaissance palazzo might exhibit Roman inscriptions and statues. The portraits included supposed makers of America—Columbus and Vespucci hung alongside Washington and Lafayette. After the Revolutionary War, Michel-Guillaume de Crèvecoeur, who had once believed that American freedom was a transplantation of England's "national genius," revised his opinion: Americans were "neither Europeans nor the descendants of Europeans" but "a new race of men." Joel Barlow, the first epic poet of independent America, hailed, "call'd from slavish chains, a bolder race." Jefferson hung his trophy hall with those un-English symbols of Pan-American patriotism. In its origins the United States resembled some of the "Latin" states far more than it resembled Canada. Like them, it was born of an improbable mating of ideas, when creolism met and married the Enlightenment.

The Spanish colonies, with their longer, stronger tradition of creole consciousness, were likely to follow the example of the northern revolutionaries; indeed, rebellions and conspiracies multiplied in the 1770s and 1780s. Soon after the emergence of the independent United States, Alejandro Malaspina, one of the new breed of scientifically trained Spanish naval officers, prepared an official fact-finding voyage across the Hispanic world. In part, it was to be Spain's answer to the great voyages of Captain Cook, Bougainville, and Pérouse—the most ambitious survey of the Americas and the Pacific ever undertaken. Indeed, the results were dazzling, commensurate with the efforts of an enlightened government, which, as Humboldt acknowledged, spent more on scientific research than any other monarchy of the day. Hundreds of thousands of samples, drawings, maps, and reports were gathered on flora, fauna, ethnography, geology, climatology, and hydrography. Yet Malaspina's brief went further: he was responsible for reporting on the political state of the empire and the best measures of reform. So much of the background of rebellion in the English colonies was also visible in those of Spain: the "creolization," the progressive delin-

eation of distinctive political identities, the political res-
tiveness, the fiscal resentment.

Spanish America was poised, for a moment, between
two possible futures. On the one hand, the future might be
as Malaspina envisioned, with authority devolved back
into provincial hands, defense costs slashed, and trade
opened to universal competition. On the other, the monarchy could continue to attempt to enforce an eighteenth-
century model of ever more rigorous centralization, with
trade regulated for the benefit of the metropolis and costly
militarization for defense, at the risk of precipitating the
kind of revolution that had already shattered Britain's
American empire. Unfortunately, Malaspina's voyage was a
long affair that outlasted the propitious moment. By the
time he returned to Spain, the French Revolution had broken out, sending frissons of horror down establishment
spines. Reform was shelved, Malaspina was disgraced, and
almost all the vast feedback of information from his scientific team was immured, unpublished, in state archives. In
America, two decades later, when the Spanish state was im-
mobilized by war, revolutions broke out that reform might
have averted.

EMERGENCE, TRANSFORMED

The independence revolutions had similar causes across
the Americas but, in important respects, differing out-
comes. In the Caribbean there was only one successful
revolution: that of Haiti. On few other islands were there
more than feeble and brief efforts to join or mimic the
continental revolutions. Canada remained aloofly loyal to
the Crown; Britain's recently acquired French subjects in

Québec evidently thought it better to be ruled from distant London than from Boston or Philadelphia. Peru and Brazil embraced independence with some reluctance. Peru's revolutionaries included reactionaries for whom the Spanish government was too liberal. Independent Brazil remained a monarchy, ruled by a scion of the royal house of the former colonial power. This was understandable, since for Brazil the Napoleonic Wars had brought the colonies closer to the mother country when the royal family had chosen exile in Brazil. For the Spanish empire, the Napoleonic invasion was an alienating experience that exposed new quarrels between the colonial and metropolitan elites. Despite the republican rhetoric that had been prominent in the rebellions, Mexico and Peru also flirted with ideas for monarchical government at intervals during the wars and after independence.

Brazilian independence came rapidly and almost bloodlessly. In the United States the war, though traumatic and divisive, was shortened by foreign help and lasted less than eight years. The Spanish colonies had no such luck; most of them were condemned to nearly two decades of destruction in merciless *guerra a muerte* against Spanish armies that demonstrated surprising resilience. I suspect, though I have seen no research to confirm it, that because they happened a generation or two later than those of North America, Spanish America's independence wars were less constrained by the enlightened, professional etiquette of the eighteenth-century battlefield. The economies of the Spanish colonies were ruined by the wars, which had caused long and total cessations of foreign trade, whereas the states of the northern Union, enjoying the benefits of protection from the French and Spanish navies, actually gained new trading partners and multiplied their shipping in the course of the war.

All the new states were riven with unresolved issues and internal rivalries but in uneven degrees. The political profile of the United States was distinctive; like Latin American countries it had federalists and anti-federalists, centralizers and particularists. But there were no conflicts of Jacobins against clericalists or absolutists against constitutionalists. The United States avoided dissolution into its constituent fragments. It made a relatively compact country, unified by good seaboard communications, with currents that all flowed northward along the coast and threaded the states together; yet even here a long, peaceful struggle was needed to impose a federalist constitution that barely kept the states together. Half-calculated ambiguities left cracks for secessionist movements, later in the new century, to widen into wounds. By good fortune, war between the states was deferred until three or four generations of peace had built up civil society and economic prosperity. Like the United States, Brazil emerged formally unified but, unlike the United States, highly fragile in the short term; the trend of offshore currents split maritime Brazil, where plantations predominated, into two zones, between which it was hard to communicate. The ranch-rich São Paulo region in the south had always been a law unto itself. And in the interior there was a "wild west" of mining, slaving, and logging with its own raffish, ungovernable boss class. Unity survived a spell of destructive civil wars in the 1830s only because the fissile regions were incapable of collaborating in revolt.

Spanish America, meanwhile, was a Humpty-Dumpty, irremediably smashed by its fall. In part this was because it

was too big, in part because it was too rich; province by
province, the elites were too big to be willing to pool patronage and power. Simón Bolívar despaired of his hopes
for postindependence unity; he had tried, he confessed, "to
plow the sea." The biggest states that emerged from the
wars—the Mexican "empire" and the united republic of
Central America—soon collapsed. Venezuela had few historic credentials for sovereignty: only as recently as 1777
it had been summoned into existence by Spanish fiat as
a subordinate administrative unit known as a captaincy-
general. The country's pretext for secession from a much
larger state created by Bolívar was that it was being treated
like a colony of "Gran Colombia" and split into small units
governed by centrally appointed intendants. Paraguay's
independence struggle was not so much against Spain—
indeed, there were hardly any hostilities there involving
royal armies—as against rival revolutionaries in Buenos
Aires. Uruguay, formerly known simply as the "East Side"
of the River Plate, originated in what was in effect a secessionist movement from fledgling Argentina, partly as a
consequence of a conflict over how centralized the postindependence constitution ought to be and partly because
Buenos Aires seemed willing to cede Uruguay to Brazil to
resolve a colonial-period territorial wrangle. The rest of
what became Argentina almost broke up because of the
mutual hatred of the river-mouth and upriver aristocracies.

It was necessarily the age of the caudillo. The United
States never experienced *caudillismo* of the Latin flavor, but
U.S. citizens of caudillo inclinations got drawn from time
to time into Latin American politics. The locus classicus is
that of Aaron Burr, who lived "a life," John Quincy Adams

said, "such as in any country of sound morals his friends would be desirous of burying in oblivion." He showed fanatical ambition and self-confidence as a child, sidestepping Princeton's admissions routine, studying sixteen hours a day when he got there, and abandoning work for idleness once he had established his intellectual reputation. The Revolutionary War made him, advancing him to the rank of colonel at little discomfort or risk and creating many opportunities of profit in his chosen profession the law—and adoptive city, New York. He became "a grave, silent, strange sort of animal" by his own appraisal. Driven by exorbitant tastes and extravagant exhibitionism but bad at business, he courted the mob. State and congressional politics whetted his appetite for power. In the New York elections of 1800 he showed himself a master of the arts of manipulating democracy—which, of course, is the best qualification for a potential dictator. He inflated his party's electoral roster by barely legal means, managed the ticket for breadth of appeal, and accused opponents of the kinds of skullduggery he committed himself. Federalists already suspected him of "meditating revolution." But like every Icarus, he overreached himself, challenging his party leader, Thomas Jefferson, for the presidency of the Union. He alienated politicians more conventional than himself, fell out with his own party, and, as his tenure as vice president neared its end in 1804, lingered in office, lamed and marginalized. Humiliatingly defeated in his bid for the governorship of New York, he avenged himself by killing the Federalist figurehead, Alexander Hamilton, in a duel. The pretext was an insult that was really no more than routine political invective—a hack journalist's claim that Burr had picked up a mistress "at a nigger ball."

Burr's debts were now so large that only an awfully big adventure could save him, his reputation so low that no risk was too daring to take. He was a believer of long standing in the reunification of the hemisphere. As early as 1796 he claimed he could "revolutionize and take possession of" South America "in its entirety." In exile from his home state, where dueling was illegal, he planned to carve himself a new niche and an enduring monument, in the style of Napoleon or Toussaint-Louverture. According to the version he divulged to the British envoy in Washington, to whom he appealed for assistance, he would bust the Union, break the Spanish monarchy, and found an empire in Spanish North America and in those western lands that were the not yet manifest destiny of the United States. Nothing came of the plan because it could not be kept secret. Burr's chief co-conspirator betrayed it. The blaze of publicity ignited the flames of a witch-hunt. Burr's arrest was ordered while he was leading an unimpressive armed expedition down the Mississippi to stage a coup in New Orleans. With calculated ambiguity, the jury found the charge of treason "not proved by any evidence submitted to us"; Burr's name remained enveloped in the smoke for the rest of his life. But he left an example of adventurism that drew imitators in subsequent generations into the maelstrom of Latin politics. This was just as well for the peace of the United States; Latin America became a safety valve where democratically uncontainable temperaments could let off steam.

The independence wars were, in short, the making of the United States and the ruin of much of the rest of the Americas. The nature of the independence struggle in Spanish America and—to some extent—of the postindependence conflict in Brazil was protracted, internecine, sanguinary, destructive, and impoverishing. To fight the wars, all the affected states had to sacrifice liberties to caudillismo and civil values to militarism. In most states the army inherited the only political legitimacy left by the wars; those who had won independence became its armed guardians. The founding constitutions echoed the enlightened rhetoric and sometimes, indeed, copied the very words of the U.S. Declaration of Independence and Constitution. But they had no opportunity to register the same effects. In cauldrons of war the ingredients of successful state making sometimes coagulate, but the longer the wars go on, the less likely that outcome. In most of the Americas in the era of independence, the pacification of society, the demythification of the leader, the submission of government to the constitution and the rule of law simply could not happen. People in the Americas often speak of the chaotic politics, democratic immaturity, and economic torpor of Latin American tradition as if they were an atavistic curse, a genetic defect, a Latin legacy. Really, like everything else in history, they are products of circumstances, and of the circumstances, in particular, in which independence was won.

INDEPENDENCE:
THE NEW
DEPENDENCY

It is hardly necessary to retrace the United States' great leap forward in the nineteenth century or recount in detail all the ways in which it took over the initiative in the Americas. A brief summary is enough to recall the well-known tally. On the eve of the period, the American Revolution, though it temporarily weakened and permanently divided Anglo-America, created a new state with unquenchable ambitions in the continental interior. In the 1790s, Britain's pincer movement on Canada's Pacific coast—by the ocean to Nootka under George Vancouver, by the pioneering transcontinental explorations of Alexander Mackenzie—transformed the grand strategic outlook. In 1803, the acquisition of the Louisiana Territory by the United States turned the infant nation into an instant giant.

In the two decades after Napoleon's invasion of Spain, Spanish America fell apart. Thereafter, the fissures continued to spread, detaching Texas and California from the Mexican state, up to the moment in the 1840s when U.S. superiority was demonstrated by the Mexican War. Most of Mexico north of the Rio Grande was annexed to Anglo-America. A historic shift had occurred; the big bucks and the big battalions were all in the north. From the sometime deserts of former barbarians, an invincibly superior people now looked down on the traditional heartlands of American civilization. U.S. citizens of a liberal disposition attacked the morality of the war, but no one doubted the outcome. Superior numbers and superior credit were bound to win—as, with rather more difficulty than was generally anticipated, they did.

After this, observers generally ceased to think of the Americas as a whole. The universal assumption was that north and south were different. Apart from the elderly lady in *Charley's Aunt* who wanted to know "In which part of the United States is Brazil?," awareness of the mutual belonging of the various parts of the Americas seemed to wither in the nineteenth century. The United States showed the world a distinctive political, economic, and cultural profile. Though Canada and Brazil were also examples of cohesive continental states, the United States was truly "united" by comparison with the fragmentary and sometimes fissile states that succeeded the Spanish empire. On the whole, the United States managed to stay at peace with the rest of Anglo-America, whereas Spanish-American states tended to fight among themselves. Except in the relatively brief period of the Civil War and the early aberration known as the Ohio-Michigan War, the United States was remarkable for political stability and nonviolent changes of government— advantages of which most Spanish-American republics seemed incapable for much of the time. The United States expanded its territory rapidly and on a grand scale at intervals throughout the century, whereas except in marginal cases, most Latin American republics had attained their potential limits by the time of independence.

In every department of economic life, the countries of Latin America receded in relative stature, while the United States towered. The educational institutions of Latin American countries, which had produced scholars and scientists of great eminence in the colonial era, stagnated, while some of those of the United States rose to what would now be called "world class." A similar reversal characterized the arts. Above all, by the crudest and most effective measure of success, the United States became an unbeatable power in war in its own hemisphere and bade fair to challenge the powers of the Old World. These changes amounted to an inversion of what had previously been American "normalcy": the common history of the hemisphere became divergent; and the centers of initiative shifted to the formerly unfavored north.

Meanwhile, partly as cause, partly as consequence of these changes, the United States followed a political and economic trajectory different from and quantifiably better than those of Latin America. The key processes—on which most of the Americas missed out—were democratization and industrialization.

In the nineteenth century every available model of the state was more or less monstrous. If the authoritarian state was a Leviathan seeking whom it might devour, democracy was a fearsome chimera with too many heads. It was particularly unsuitable for those parts of the Americas where there were huge Native American and slave populations that would outvote the traditional political nations. In much of Latin America, even the northern model of a racially selective democracy, which excluded blacks and corralled Indians in reservations, was impracticable. Miscegenation had already created too many racial classifications; it was impossible to identify a racially defined political class; and *hacenderos* needed their Indians where they could exploit their labor without conceding too many inconvenient rights. Latin American constitutions could be profligate with the franchise only if people were not allowed to exercise it. Real democracy, with genuinely universal suffrage, lots of local devolution or "subsidiarity," and broad, committed participation has been slow in the making, even in the United States, which is its homeland and its forge. It is still imperfect: the ballot is abandoned by millions of people and bought by millions of dollars; elections are despised by many and "stolen" by a few. To write the true history of democracy in the United States, a historian would have to get beyond the narrative of the Constitution and the tally of the franchise and go "down on the farm" and into the forums where democratic relationships were made: the church halls, wagon trains, and whalers; the school yards and buses, camps and clambakes, baseball grounds and hot-dog stands. It was the abundance of such forums, and their proliferation, that made the United States precocious in democracy. Latin America was deficient, on the whole, not in formal constitutional provisions for voting, or in democratic rhetoric, but in the actual spaces where shared identities could be forged among people of different classes.

By the time Tocqueville researched *Democracy in America*, the United States had an exemplary democratic franchise (except in Rhode Island, where property qualifications for voters were still fairly stringent) in the sense that almost all adult white males had the vote. Tocqueville was wise enough, however, to realize that democracy really meant something deeper and subtler than that. He was the first ethnographer of a complex society. He was a pioneer revisionist for democracy in an age of reaction, when most men of his class still felt the terror of the tumbrils and the menace of the mob. Democracy, he concluded, was inevitable. "The same democracy reigning in American societies" was "advancing rapidly toward power in Europe," and the obligation of the old ruling class was to adapt accordingly: "to instruct democracy, reanimate its beliefs, purify its mores, regulate its movements"—in short, to tame it without destroying it. Most constitutional reformers were mindful of Aristotle's doctrine that democracy degenerates into anarchy and leads to tyranny; indeed, the tragic course of the French Revolution seemed to have proved them right. For Tocqueville, however, democracy, if properly domesticated and civilized, could be a means to Utopia: "a society which all, regarding the law as their work, would love and submit to without trouble," where "each having rights and being assured of preserving his rights, a manly confidence and a sort of reciprocal condescension between the classes would be established, as far from haughtiness as from baseness." Meanwhile, "the free association of citizens" would "shelter the state from both tyranny and licence."

America never perfectly exemplified the theory. Tocqueville was frank about the shortcomings of the American experiment, some of which are still evident today: the costliness and inefficiency of government, the venality and ignorance of many public officials; the high levels of political bombast; the tendency for conformism to counterbalance individualism; the menace of an intellectually feeble pantheism; the peril of the "tyranny of the majority"; the tension between crass materialism and religious enthusiasm; the threat from a rising plutocracy that could gain control of the state. Henry Clay spotted Andrew Jackson as a potential Bonaparte, "a mere military chieftain" with a record as a fighter in street brawls and frontier wars. Jackson's inauguration evoked in onlookers "the reign of King Mob." He diverted power to a "Kitchen Cabinet." He used his veto to override Congress and the Supreme Court. His success as a demagogue kept him faithful to the electoral process, and he was able to retire, like an ancient dictator, undefeated from office. He then regretted not hanging or shooting his political adversaries when he had the chance.

Nevertheless, the advantages of democracy outweighed the defects. They could be computed in dollars and cents and measured in splendid monuments erected in newly transformed wildernesses. Achievements included the strength of civic spirit, the spread of respect for law, the prospect of material progress, and above all, the liberation of effort and energy that results from equality of opportunity. The United States was protected from *caudillismo* by the real stuff of democracy: indifference to heroes, except in fiction—or, rather, a conviction that heroism has its own sphere. Successful generals often became elected commander in chief, like Zachary Taylor, "who did his own darning . . . and who could lead men to their death." Ulysses S. Grant was more a workhorse than a warhorse. They appealed rather as organizers, logistically efficient, than as "men of destiny." The first Japanese ambassador to the United States was shocked to find that no one knew who the descendants of George Washington were or where they lived. In the land of Sulla and Cincinnatus, the man on horseback dismounts. The U.S. president is commander in chief of the armed forces. This constitutional convention, which caps the forces with a civil, democratically elected officer, is one of the devices that protects the United States from coups, whereas in other parts of the Americas, the separation of supreme authority in the state from supreme authority in the military encourages "men on horseback" to "pronounce." If all citizens accepted military discipline, society would be militarized and democracy outflanked. Tocqueville took it for granted that the American system was the source of American success.

There was, however, another source, complementary and equally essential: industrialization. Latin American countries tended to remain economically dependent on monocultures or on a few primary products, while the United States experienced an industrial revolution. From an economic point of view, the early nineteenth century was probably a bad time to gain independence. Free trade, which was a shibboleth of the independence revolutionaries throughout the Americas, favored industrializing economies that produced cheap goods and condemned the Latin American states, which emerged as fully free-market players in that era for the first time, to underdevelopment; they could not catch up with the industrial revolutions of Europe and North America and so became locked into a role as producers of primary products for other people's industrialization: the metals and timber and rubber that supplied the factories; the foods and fertilizers that went to feed the workforces; the opiates that dulled their senses; the stimulants that fought their need for sleep; the sweets that kept their blood sugar up. Where there were plenty of Indians, coolies, and slaves, mechanization was a waste of capital. In the labor-hungry United States, outside the slave states, it was a necessity. The United States had hardly any dependent peasants. Its small farmers were their own bosses; its big farmers and ranchers used mobile labor. Large parts of Latin America could not be pried from big *hacenderos,* running their establishments with Indian peons or—if Indians were unavailable—coolie gangs. Landlord-oligarchs ruled or sponsored rulers who ruled in their interests.

Once industrialization was under way, it opened a wealth gap between North America and the rest that has grown ever since and is only beginning to narrow today. One way of measuring it is through the statistics of immigration, the phenomenon that remade the United States. Between 1890 and 1920 migration brought the United States a net gain of over eighteen million people—more than in the entire previous history of the country and more than three times that of the whole of Latin America put together.

There were lots of civil wars in the nineteenth century; what made the United States' special was that it happened in an industrializing context. It was unlike those of Latin America, more like the contemporary civil wars of Germany, Italy, and Japan. In all these conflicts of the 1860s, a common pattern prevailed. Industrializing regions imposed on unindustrializing neighbors and created centralized political systems, fueled and furthered by the resources that industrialization made possible: technologically advanced armies and police; mass-produced munitions; rapid communications; well-equipped bureaucracies; highly mobile free labor; intensive, mechanized food production and distribution. In all these conflicts, old-fashioned agrarian societies—like the Confederacy with its planters and slaves—succumbed to the industrializing giants: Prussia in Germany's wars of unity, Piedmont in Italy's Risorgimento, Choshu and Satsuma in Japan's Meiji Restoration, and the Union in the American Civil War. No Latin American civil war could have had the same structure or the same sort of outcome.

By the time of the Civil War, industrialization in the United States was already creating a further, farther-reaching effect. It was making a massive agricultural revolution possible. The colonization of the North American prairie and the conversion of this vast area, once known as the Great American Desert, into the granary of the world and an arena of cities is arguably the biggest modification of the natural environment ever achieved in the course of human history. The North American Midwest never experienced the long period of glaciation that preceded the forests and shaped the soil. Virtually nothing grew naturally that human stomachs could digest; except in a few relatively small patches, the unyieldingly tough soils could not be broken without industrial technology. Even as late as 1827, when James Fenimore Cooper wrote *The Prairie*, it seemed a place without a future, "a vast country, incapable of sustaining a dense population." Then steel plows began to bite into sods too tough to yield to earlier farming technologies. Rifled guns drove off the natives and killed off the undomesticable fauna—the great buffalo herds. Cheap nails and machined planks made it possible to erect balloon-framed, "Chicago-built" cities in treeless places. Railroads could carry the grain to where it was salable. Grain elevators, introduced in 1850, made it possible to grow and store the grains without vast amounts of labor. Giant flour mills processed them into marketable wares. Wheat was the edible grass, new to the region, that made the land yield efficient plant food for humans.

By the time Anthony Trollope saw it in 1861, the prairie had already been transformed into the most productive source of food in the world. He was stupefied by the quantities of grain—sixty million bushels transported via Buffalo in a single year—and "grieved by the loose manner in which wheat was treated" in Minnesota—"bags of it upset and left upon the ground. The labor of collecting it was more than it was worth." The domestication of the prairie made the United States and Canada genuinely world powers, with influence over the price of food. They became truly continent-wide countries. Among the consequences was that the most underexploited of North America's resources—space—was put to productive use. The resource gap that had formerly made societies richer in middle America and parts of South America had already narrowed and begun to reverse. The conquest of a hostile environment opened an unbridgeable gap in the North's favor.

Latin America could not perform this miracle. There were great grasslands in the south, in Patagonia, the pampa and the *sertão*, and except in scale, they resemble the North American prairie physically. But they never had the great living resource that made the prairie a hunter's paradise: the American bison. Pampa dwellers had the guanaco to live off, but they were poor beasts by comparison, too small to yield the ample stores of meat or the great hides for dwellings that were the "buffalo's" gift, or the large amounts of leather. The southern grasslands were incorporated into the states that shared them—Argentina, Uruguay, Brazil, and Chile. But they were less extensive than the northern prairie, unable to provide adequate interim food stocks for a transition to agriculture, and poorly sited for access to major markets. In the nineteenth century they experienced no great revolution, only a gradual expansion of the kind of exploitation that was already characteristic in the late colonial period: ranching for wool and hides, products that could be stored and transported without spoiling. There was no point in developing the pampa or Patagonia for farming, or even trying to exploit the ranched animals for meat. The result would only have been to add to the Southern Hemisphere's growing surplus of meat, for which there were no accessible markets. The unplanned spread of European grasses and weeds meant that sheep and cattle could thrive, but there was too little demand within an accessible compass to build a major meat industry.

In the long run, industrialized supply solved this problem: first canning, which by the mid–nineteenth century was reliable enough to justify the creation of a corned-beef industry; then refrigeration. The first long-range shipment of frozen meat is generally said to have been made in 1876 by the S.S. *Paraguay* from Argentina to France at minus 30 degrees Celsius. The success of this enterprise, and the problems of competing with North American grains, meant that development of the grasslands of the southern cone was arrested in a pastoral phase. The gaucho lived on while the cowboy transferred to "Wild West shows" and the cinema. To this day, there are no great cities in Patagonia or the pampa, no glamorous centers of culture and civic ambition such as make the North American Midwest wonderful. The traveler still feels on a frontier; inhabitants continue a tradition of affected embarrassment at their own remoteness, sharing the shame of Nora Mackinnon, a young bride on a Patagonian *estancia* in the 1950s, who tried to keep up appearances when a director's wife visited by dressing for dinner and getting a half-trained servant to hand the vegetables—"a roast potato rolled into a silken lap." The Argentinian grasslands remained home to ruminants; only recently and gradually have maize and wheat come to be exploited on a large scale. This is still ranchers' grassland, where there are few substantial markets near at hand and meat processing is the main industry.

PARALLEL HISTORIES IN THE NINETEENTH-CENTURY AMERICAS

But even in the nineteenth century, the divergence of the history of the United States from the hemispheric pattern has probably been exaggerated. It can be selectively tested by a few comparisons in areas commonly assumed to be divergent. The key areas can be labeled as: the fabric of dependency, which, contrary to common assumptions, was not a peculiarly Latin American problem; the continuing pursuit of the frontier, which was not a North American prerogative but a theme in the history of almost all the continental states; the fate of the Native American peoples; and the common features of American popular religion. It is worth looking at each of these in turn, starting with dependency.

Most attempted explanations of Latin America's arrestation boil down to blame: if Latin Americans suffer from arrested development, it is their own fault for being Latin or Catholic or both. "Temperament" and mind-set—addiction to an authoritarianism incompatible with democracy and hostile to economic freedoms—have held them back. The most popular alternative theory simply reverses the blame. Outside the United States and Canada, the Americas have been checked by dependency, their development stunted by a series of colonial and neocolonial relationships. The imperialism of European powers—mainly Spain and Portugal—was succeeded by British "business imperialism" and gringo hegemony.

The fit with the facts is pretty loose. Although in the colonial period the colonies were clearly "dependent," in some degree, on metropolitan decision makers, economic retardation was not among the results. For most of the Americas, colonial rule had coincided with the age of sail. Communications across the Atlantic were slow and unpredictable. Empires were hard to integrate economically, and geographically specialized production was impracticable for many goods of high-volume demand. Although metropolitan powers usually wanted to restrain colonial industries in favor of their own manufactures, this was hard to achieve in practice. The British did so in nineteenth-century India, but that was in an industrializing era, when British industries had the advantages of mechanized production and increasingly, as the century went on, steam-powered transport. These advantages were unavailable during the colonial period in the Americas. The Spanish colonies had far more trade with one another than with the mother country (though in Brazil's case the situation was different: the various provinces had little contact even with one another, and almost all outward traffic was normally routed via Portugal). The colonial relationship was a stimulus to the creation of native industries rather than a source of inhibition. What would now be called import substitution was normal; the imports that could not be satisfactorily produced in situ tended to be those brought across the Pacific from the Philippines—Chinese silks and the spiceries and pharmaceuticals of the "spice islands"—rather than the manufactures of Spain.

On the other hand, the New World colonies had a big and valuable range of primary or semiprocessed products that could not be adequately supplied from elsewhere to Old World markets: silver, sugar, cotton, tobacco, hardwoods, chocolate, cochineal, salt cod, whaling products. These goods ensured that most colonies for most of the time had a favorable trade balance and were able to accumulate capital for investment. Colonialism, moreover, stimulated the economy by introducing new means of wealth creation: ranching, large-scale mining, plantations and huge numbers of slaves to work them; it also provided a network of commerce and exchange of enormous reach, unimaginable before the Europeans arrived. The diseases that arrived in the New World along with the rest of the ecological package wrought havoc on the indigenous labor force, but the economic effects of this were mixed. Most indigenous communities found it hard to adapt to the new economic opportunities of the colonial era; their labor played, in any event, a relatively small part. Imported slaves made up for some of the population loss and could be concentrated where they were most useful. The millions of deaths encouraged economical, laborsaving activities (which, in theory, ought to have included mechanization). Death can be profitable. In general, the colonial era must be acknowledged as a great source of economic promotion and innovation all over the Americas. Technical improvements and capital accumulation, the universal prerequisites of economic growth, were available in unprecedented abundance.

Nineteenth-century forms of dependency worked rather differently once most of the hemisphere had established independence, by the late 1820s. It would be naïve to suppose that colonialism had been eradicated. The elites of the independence era became the imperialists in their own hinterlands, conquering and exploiting indigenous peoples. European capitalism muscled in with investments, strings attached. This "business imperialism" was again, however, a common history experienced by the Americas as a whole and cannot be invoked to explain the peculiar fortunes of any particular part. If anything, the United States had an advantage in attracting massive British investment in its industrial infrastructure ahead of the rest of the Americas. During the period 1870–1914, the United States and Canada were easily the biggest destinations per capita of foreign investment in the world. Britain—always peculiarly a potent source of capital for other countries, presumably because of British capitalists' lack of confidence in their own—owned huge swathes of the Americas in the late nineteenth and early twentieth centuries, accounting for over half the foreign investment in Latin America and an even greater proportion in the United States. British investment fever in U.S. opportunities during the colonization of the "Wild West" sank many fortunes and provided satirical fodder for Dickens in *Martin Chuzzlewit* and Trollope in *The Way We Live Now*. The reason for this needs more research, but it is a fair guess that British investors were culturally prejudiced in favor of North American opportunities.

Dependent relationships, in any case, crisscrossed the hemisphere. In the United States the postbellum South had a dependent relationship with the North—a situation that endured for a hundred years after the Civil War. Had the outcome of the war been different, or had the North not ventured to reconquer the South, there would presumably be a big "Anglo" state in North America to this day with a dependent system resembling the classic pattern: a relatively small, rich elite of consumers wasting resources on fancy imports, with little incentive to diversify or industrialize; a racially differentiated class of poor, condemned to poverty by the surplus of labor; a highly vulnerable and unstable pattern of exports based on a few key crops; and reliance on foreign merchants and shippers with consequently prolific leaching of the export-trade profits. Some of the products of the independence era were different, but the Old World still needed the New, and now more than ever, for previously underexploited products such as coffee, rubber, guano, copper, nitrates, wool, hides, salt, canned meat, and—by the end of the century—frozen meat. Except in the minds of fantasists, "gunboat diplomacy" played little part in influencing the economic policies of American countries or enforcing unfair terms of trade.

THE FRONTIER

Nor was the United States America's only homegrown empire in the nineteenth century. Brazil, too, had an empire on her doorstep—an interior of underexploited promise, inhabited by expendable natives. Brazil also had an informal overseas empire of her own; Angola—the prime supplier of her slaves—and, for a while, Portugal itself were among her dependencies. Successive Portuguese governments feared that Brazil would take over such Portuguese colonies as remained in Africa and the East. Brazil resisted the temptation but only because a vast hinterland of her own still awaited exploration and exploitation. "With regard to colonies on the coast of Africa," declared the first ruler of independent Brazil, "we want none; nor anywhere else; Brazil is quite large enough and productive enough for us, and we are content with what Providence has given us."

In short, Brazil's hinterland was its empire and the forest its frontier. Historians now apply frontier theory to Latin American history; it was the subject of a pioneering book by Alistair Hennessy as long ago as 1970. But the notion that the frontier is peculiarly or particularly a North American phenomenon remains influential. The histories of the United States and Canada seem to lend themselves to frontier theory. They are broad, squat countries with widely separated seaboards. For both, the forge of nationhood was the wilderness in the middle, which pioneers and settlers had to cross. Their trailblazing histories became cherished national myths, impressed on retinas by the

Golden Age of Hollywood. In this dangerous land, there was "no time to delay/So whipcrackaway!" The vast frontier was a peculiar kind of moral and social environment. Law was morally compromised—with professional gunslingers recycled as town sheriffs or "Pinkertons," while U.S. marshals paid fleeting visits. Conflicts were rife: with Indians, ideal subjects for tragedy, who inspired pity and fear by turns; or between "the cowman and the farmer," who should be friends; or between the herders of cattle and sheep; or between claim stakers and land-grabbers in ill-organized races for property rights; or disputes over water rights and railroad corridors; or struggles with the omnipresent outlaw. The foci of battle were evanescent: the corral of wagons, which would move on—Indians permitting   at dawn; the cavalry stockade, which would be relocated as crisis succeeded crisis; the frontier town, which could be transformed into a "ghost town" with stunning rapidity. Short-lived histories, like those of the stagecoach companies and the Pony Express, assumed disproportionate magnetism in the mythopoeia of dime novels and B movies. Here prowess, heroism, and mutual help were necessary for survival, let alone victory.

The story lasted throughout the formative period of the history of the independent Americas, from the 1790s, when transcontinental exploration began to trace the trails, until the 1890s, when America's ends were tied together by prolific rail traffic along just about every exploitable route and middle America was filled with new ways of life that made it culturally consistent—albeit not uniform—with the seaboards. Frederick Jackson Turner, perhaps the most influential historian the United States has seen, turned the myth into a sort of science. Frontiers were socially and institutionally creative because they attracted vanguards and opened up gaps between metropolis and march—generational gaps, because the young went to the frontier; social gaps, because the frontier drew the outcasts and the entrepreneurs; wealth gaps, because the frontier was a land of opportunity; political gaps, because the frontier was tough, cultivating individualism while valuing order, reconciling radicalism and conservatism, and promoting particularism and democracy because there was nothing else to do. Frontiers left central governments and aristocracies behind. These effects modified the old world of the eastern seaboard in turn, keeping America young and roping it to frontiersmen's love of freedom, democracy, and solidarity.

Of course, there was more to it than that, crucially, in four ways. First, American history was not a unilinear *Drang nach Westen;* rather, it is grid-shaped. The United States was also built by northward movement from the south, cultural oscillations across the Spanish borderlands. H. E. Bolton, who pioneered the exploration of this important fact, never succeeded in displacing from American minds Jackson's model of the making of America, but he supervised more Ph.D. theses than any other American historian. Thanks in part, no doubt, to the current demographic rehispanization of much of the North American Southwest, borderland research is now a huge industry within historical scholarship, generating some of the best work in the world. What it is revealing is the map of the northward spread of missions and presidios in a barely interrupted history, which began with the conquest of New Mexico in 1598 and has resumed with the cross-border migrancy of our own times.

Second, according to frontier theory, the story is about generation gaps and the cultivation of distinctive mentalities, but the crude history of the frontier is of the expropriation of indigenous peoples and the bloody resolution of border disputes. Officially, the frontier was always a zone marked down in the ledgers for cultural homogenization; the only exception was made for the Indians, and the U.S. government has wavered even on that point, tacking between policies of separation and integration. In 1872, the U.S. secretary of the interior foretold the future he expected for the Indians, extolling "our duty to coerce them, if necessary, into the adoption and practice of our habits and customs," and though the federal government revised the policy of enforced integration at intervals—notably in the 1930s and 1960s—distinctive indigenous cultures have withered, in practice, almost to the point of extinction. "Indian rights" today usually means the right to exploit gambling casinos, golf courses, and shopping malls.

Third, the Americas collectively remained a frontier from a European perspective. Immigrants forged national consciousness against the odds in surprising places: whaling ships, wagon trains, school buses, night classes, army camps, baseball grounds, hot-dog stands. Though the United States and Canada were the biggest magnets for migrants until the United States began to introduce strict controls in the 1890s, most of the continental republics and Cuba all made huge net gains of population in the late nineteenth and early twentieth centuries; in Brazil, Uruguay, and Argentina the provenance of the newcomers was as diverse as for Canada and the United States.

Finally, the frontier was not uniquely North American. Frontier effects characterized the making of other American states. We have had glimpses, in the course of this book, of how frontier expansion continued into the era of independence: Argentina's in the pampa and Patagonia, Chile's in Araucania, Brazil's in Amazonia, and Mexico's in its nineteenth- and twentieth-century struggles to control its own Indian territories, north and south, where Yaqui and Maya respectively fought long wars against the state. In many of these cases and others like them, the process involved the domestication and adaptation for new economic activities of previously underexploited environments. Dramatic instances of the frontier effect continued into the twentieth century, when newly arrived migrant communities brought distinctive ways of life—austere moralities, unconventional ways of organizing families: the Mennonites in the Chaco, Japanese utopians in the Brazilian forest, Welsh escapees from English imperialism in Patagonia, "Aryan" racists seeking to preserve their own purity in lands too remote and unwanted to be disturbed.

THE PEOPLES BEYOND THE FRONTIERS

The frontier was a brave new world with people in it. The story of the nineteenth-century Americas is, in part, a story of conflict between those people and the expanding new states. It was an unequal struggle, always settled in favor of the invaders. But that does not mean that it should be told as a fable with an easy moral. There were neither superior nor inferior peoples in conflict, neither pure victors nor mere victims. The story of the conquest of the grasslands from their native peoples, for instance, is best understood as a clash of competing imperialisms—indigneous imperialists pitted against imperialists from outside.

The histories of the North American prairie and the South American grasslands really began to converge when Europeans introduced cattle and sheep, multiplying available stores of meat. At least as significant were the horses Europeans brought to pampa and prairie alike; native peoples adopted them and adapted their ways of life to them. The result was the rise of more efficient hunting cultures, pastoral societies, and predatory imperialists capable of controlling great swathes of grassland. They arose first in the pampa in the mid–eighteenth century, when some local leaders began to absorb lessons in large-scale chieftaincy from the Araucanos, the impressive warriors of southern Chile, who maintained effective independence beyond the reach of the Spanish empire. On the rivers Negro and Colorado, Cacapol, "the Attila of the Pampa," turned his role as an elected war chief into a hereditary monarchy. With his son, Cangapol "el Bravo," he organized a lucrative trade in guanaco pelts, assembled harems of a size suited to chiefly status, raised thousands of warriors, threatened Buenos Aires, and impressed visiting Jesuits.

By the end of the century a similar phenomenon was visible in the prairie: the rise of the Sioux. They were a former forest people, eighteenth-century converts to nomadism and a horseborne way of life. They conquered the Black Hills—their "meat store"—from the Kiowa, Cheyenne, and Crow, with an ideology of violence and the aid of the great microbial ally of modern imperialism: smallpox. They preyed on the sedentary world of the upper Missouri. The white man did not introduce imperialism to the Great Plains; he arrived as a competitor with a Sioux empire that was already taking shape.

The outcome was predictable. The indigenous imperialists of pampa and plain faced insuperable military technology; in the late nineteenth century the technology gap that favored the "tools of empire" was at its widest. General John Pope vowed utterly to exterminate the Sioux "as maniacs or wild beasts"; they proved surprisingly hard to defeat on the battlefield but were crushed by attrition—

their lands carved by railways, their reservations broken up, their communities harassed by exemplary massacres. Doles of cattle bought off the survivors. Similar ruthlessness solved the corresponding problem in Argentina. Domingo Faustino Sarmiento had already decided in the 1840s, before the formulation of Darwinism, that Argentina's indigenous peoples were doomed "to disappear from the face of the earth" by white competition. In the 1880s, General Roca's machine guns fulfilled his prophecy.

Meanwhile, final frontiers were falling in the boreal north and Antarctic south of the hemisphere. Along with grassland, the environments most closely mirrored in both moieties of the Americas are tundra and taiga. America is an asymmetrical hemisphere. Most of its land lies to the north, while most of its people live toward the south. The main reason for this is climatic. North America is skewed toward the cold. The continent seems to spread and fan outward as it approaches and enters the Arctic, whereas it tapers and tails off as it approaches the Antarctic. The hemisphere's only ice dwellers live in the north. But in the extreme south of Patagonia and parts of Tierra del Fuego there is a world of cold scrub and dwarf birchlands that bears direct comparison with corresponding environments in North America. It is a relatively small area, relatively more exposed, over more of its extent, to contacts with the cultures of neighboring environments. Whereas the North American tundra is heavily belted with boreal forest, there is very little of this in the south. As usual, the north has a monopoly of land-based big game. The caribou and musk ox—the magnets that drew hunting peoples to these latitudes in the first place—make a huge difference to the material culture of the Athabaskan speakers who predominate at the northern end of the boreal forests, compared with the guanaco, which, until European livestock arrived, were the main land-based protein source for people in Tierra del Fuego and Patagonia. In some places in the north, copper and meteoric iron were available for tools. Where lake and marine resources supplemented the forest, North America, around parallel 55, offered more abundance to its traditional inhabitants than did its mirror world in the south.

The cold, sparsely populated extremities of the hemisphere have one thing more in common. They are magnets for study: the north, in search of an explanation and account of the first peopling of the hemisphere; the south, because it was here that Darwin met the Fuegians and began his reflections on the place of man in evolution. The Fuegians startled Darwin by their indifference to cold, which they faced naked at temperatures that compelled Europeans to put on every available layer of clothes; it made him wonder whether their metabolisms had adapted to their environment. If so, they did so early; the earliest archaeological evidence of human settlement in Tierra del Fuego has been found at altitudes over two thousand feet above sea level. In favored coastal patches, winter temperatures hover around freezing and soar up to 80 degrees F. in summer, a climate less extreme than that of New York and considerably more favorable than that of southern Patagonia. Tierra del Fuego has less severe winters, more rain, greener pastures, fatter guanaco.

On the basis of his observations in Tierra del Fuego, Darwin formulated the opinion that "when two races meet, they act precisely like two species of animals. They fight each other." The subsequent history of the island grimly illustrated his conviction that in such encounters the "white races" would always win the struggle for survival of the fittest. In the 1880s alluvial gold was discovered and sheep farming began. The natives were in the way, and to exterminate them, professional man hunters arrived—"white Indians" like Julio Popper, a failed miner, or a marksman called MacLennan, who charged one pound per Indian and earned £412 in a year. Sam Ishlop, one of the most successful exterminators, routinely tortured his victims and specialized in the rape murder of virgins. Colonial administrators frankly accepted such activities as mildly regrettable necessities. The Salesian Fathers, who established missions in 1889 and 1896, had some success in deterring the man hunters but could not protect the natives from the equally fatal ravages of disease. The farms owned by the exemplary Bridges family offered similar inadequate refuges for imperiled natives. In 1880, by the missionaries' reckoning, 3,500 Selk'nam and Haush were left alive, alongside about 7,500 of the "canoe people," the Yamaná and Alakaluf. Only 84 Selk'nam still lived in 1924. By 1980 only one Selk'nam descendant survived, plus five mestizos on Great Island. Thus this most extraordinary of American environments, which, through its influence on Darwin, has so powerfully affected the world, ended up registering a common American experience: European inruption, indigenous obliteration.

BLACK HISTORY

If Native Americans had a common history in the nineteenth century, so did blacks: a history of emancipation from slavery and of struggle with racism. As they were liberated from an old form of oppression, they were victimized by a new one. Slavery became uneconomical, superannuated, rationally unsustainable. But even as it withered, pseudoscientific racism arose, restacking the world in order of race, locating blacks at the bottom and justifying oppression as the due reward of inherent inferiority, measured by craniological computations, crushed to fit distorted Darwinism.

Vermont was the first place in the Americas to free the slaves, adopting in 1774 a principle that, in England, Lord Mansfield had declared in a famous judgment: slavery was incompatible with English common law. Vermont had few slaves and so could afford the luxury of this logic. In most of the Americas slaves were freed at or soon after independence, but this should not be mistaken for revolutionary adherence to the language of liberty. Roughly speaking, emancipation occurred in order of the importance of slaves in the economies of the places concerned or the esteem for slavery in their cultures. Meanwhile, the slave trade was being abolished in law and eroded in practice, as British gunboats tried to enforce what would now be called an ethical foreign policy. The U.S. Navy collaborated in this British endeavor, even though slavery remained legal in much of the Union; this was not inconsistent, according to the logic of the time. The trade was vitiated by peculiar iniquities—the evils of enslavement by kidnapping and war, the inhumanities of the transatlantic passage, the splitting of families; the institution itself, however, was hallowed by antiquity and intellectually separable from such side issues as whether slaves were well treated or how far they should enjoy rights protected by law. Almost every known human society has practiced slavery in some form. To do without it was a most extraordinary notion. Two supposed natural laws—to liberty and to property—were in conflict, and there was no easy way of resolving it theoretically. Moral crusaders concentrated on trying to eliminate the trade, believing that the institution would wither in consequence. In fact, interference with the trade inaugurated a golden age for the slavers as prices rose. In some slave-owning societies, masters got their slaves to breed; the prospect arose that slavery could be self-perpetuating.

After independence, slavery continued to overlap different parts of the hemisphere, though as time went on the differences in the way the institution worked grew more various from place to place. In the United States most slave owners managed relatively small numbers—a tenth on average in Virginia of the average in Jamaica at emancipation. In the mid–nineteenth century only six of the fifteen slave states of the Union had a black population approaching or exceeding half the total. In all but two others the proportion was less than a quarter. In Brazil and Cuba at the time, whites formed a minority. In former Spanish colonies, slavery on a large scale was highly localized; the plantation economy was confined to coastal areas of the mainland and to the Atlantic islands. Though mining relied heavily on slaves in early days, wage labor gradually took over.

All the continental republics except Paraguay, where slavery remained lawful until 1869, imposed emancipation before the United States. So did most of the Caribbean imperial territories. In Puerto Rico slavery lingered into the 1870s and in Cuba and Brazil into the 1880s. Territories where the slave trade was admitted longest had the largest numbers of freedmen and, paradoxically perhaps, experienced faster racial integration, with a higher incidence of mixed marriage, than the United States. U.S. owners, who found it hard to elude the antislavers' blockades, changed their policies and began successfully breeding slaves at home by encouraging marriage and family life and creating the paternalistic world of Uncle Tom. The antislavery movement had no answer to this demographic formula, or to slave cultures' indifference to the market forces that were supposed to make slavery obviously unprofitable. So it took a war to emancipate the slaves. Even then, Lincoln "would have kept slavery" to save the Union, if he could. In the hectic conditions of the conquest of the Confederacy, power over the slaves passed into the hands of local Union commanders. Some enforced slavery in order to appease enemies; some suspended it in order to gain recruits. In the end, slavery crumbled piecemeal, unplanned, as—in effect—countless local orders abolished it. Racism, instead of slavery, became the "peculiar institution" of the Old South as defeated elites passed segregation laws and enshrined discrimination to protect themselves from a newly emancipated underclass.

The social and cultural effects of slavery were still profound wherever they happened, but they took new forms; the African feel of the colonial plantations gradually dispersed. Outside the North American South, populations blended. But distinctively black culture survived, especially in religion. The proof is strikingly clear for Brazil, where only 5 percent of the population is now registered as black but where the number of descendants of black slaves is, in both absolute and relative terms, the highest in the hemisphere. Black religion thrives. Pagan religiosity survives with African roots. In Bahía it is called Candomblé, Xungó in Pernambuco, Umbanda in Maranhão, and macumba in Rio. The essential rites are everywhere the same: spirit possession, "lending bodies to the gods." Under the advocation of the Queen of the Sea, the Blessed Virgin doubles as Iemanjá, an African sea goddess. Thunderous Saint Barbara becomes the wife of the Yoruba thunder god, Xango. Their worshipers "call" them with the aid of blood offerings and magic diagrams chalked on the temple floor. There are one thousand Candomblé temples in Bahía, four thousand African cult centers in all. The affectation of hysterical behavior in pursuit of a trance— including giggling, babbling, and uncontrolled dancing— helps, perhaps, to explain the growing appeal of charismatic Christian worship in Brazil. During or after trances, mediums provide consultations, usually enveloped in rum fumes and cigar smoke. The language of the worshipers is full of echoes of Africa, for "Africa," says one of the most famous macumba priestesses, "is the land of life."

THE AMERICAN CENTURY

In the twentieth century the United States became a motor of global culture, exporting tastes, styles, looks, foods, and sounds all over the world and transforming other cultures into its image by the power of its magnetism. Military clout is a grim way of reckoning the virtue of a state, but it is at least objectively testable; by this standard, the United States grew crushingly dominant as its military budget came to dwarf those of all rivals in combination. By the end of the century, there was no contest: the United States had seen off all competitors for power. Anyone who wanted another model of how to run a country had to imagine it: the "third way," the "Asian way"—notional alternatives, never exemplified. The spread of American models was enormously stimulated by the power of international business. Most major multinational companies were based in the States, about a quarter of them (excluding banks) in the 1990s. The United States became, by the end of the millennium, the world's only superpower: homeland of the biggest economy in the world, the biggest market, the biggest producer, the "global policeman," the powerhouse that drives the economies of other countries. It was home to some of the world's most prodigious collections of art. Here were the world's most potent educational institutions, a nursery of genius and talent about as productive as the world had ever seen, rivaling or excelling the China of the Hundred Schools, the Athens of Plato and Aristotle, the Florence of the Quattrocento. Except perhaps in the arts, the United States remained disproportionately dominant in the Americas, in all the achievements in which Americans have excelled.

Even more remarkably, this ascent was achieved without much sacrifice of democracy. All the other states that contended for unique superpower status in the same period—Germany, Russia, Japan, China—did so with absolutist or totalitarian regimes, with their promise of maximized efficiency and the ruthless subordination of means to ends. We can imagine historians of the future dating the decline of the United States from around or soon after the turn of the millennium, but at that moment—a moment of climax, perhaps of culmination, a peak from which the only way was down—this "America" was the cynosure and in some degree the pattern of the world. For a state founded on usurpation, nurtured through conflict, developed in slavery, and expanded at its victims' expense, this is an amazing record.

Inevitably, against this background, in the Americas the twentieth century was marked by gringo supremacy. It is not convincing, however, to blame this circumstance for the continuing retardation of development in the Americas outside the United States. Nor should we assume that the rest of the hemisphere is permanently disqualified from catching up. If the twentieth century was "American" by virtue of U.S. preponderance, the twenty-first may be American, too, in a fuller sense of the word.

THE IMPERIAL REPUBLIC

When the twentieth century began, the United States was already, in effect, an empire, gobbling up a lot of other people's territory and beginning to develop the "business imperialism" of overseas investment. The country was already the homeland of a land empire, formed mainly by expansion into contiguous areas at the expense of their former occupants—"Red Indians," Mexicans, Canadians, and complaisant Russians. Secessionist regions were forced to stay in the Union, without reference to what would later be called "rights of self-determination." This was not a conventional empire on the European maritime model but resembled some land empires created by similar means—those, for example, conquered in the eighteenth century by the Dutch in the hinterlands of their maritime establishments in Java, or by Russians in Central Asia, Siberia, and eastern Europe, or by Russia's successor state, the Soviet Union.

When the land frontier officially "closed" in 1896, American imperialism spilled into the ocean, that "wider field" for the "exercise" of "American intellect" of which Turner wrote. It looked as if America was bound for a future as yet one more white imperial power among many—"a power among the nations of the world," as Joseph B. Foraker said, that "wants colonial possessions." The United States acquired the Philippines, Guam, Puerto Rico, and Guantánamo Bay (1898), Hawaii and American Samoa (1899), the Panama Canal Zone and a protectorate over Cuba (1903). Nicaragua was occupied in 1912, and Haiti, the Dominican Republic, and Cuba were all taken under American control during the First World War. Denouncing this record to President Woodrow Wilson, the prominent Argentine intellectual Manuel Ugarte said the Stars and Stripes had become "a symbol of oppression." At about the same time, the Virgin Islands, the last territorial acquisition, were bought from Denmark and became U.S. territory.

Most of the U.S. empire, therefore, was still inside the Americas. "Backyard" security, at least as much as imperial vainglory, was the reason for acquiring it and replacing it, as and when occupied territories were returned, with indirect forms of empire. Short of direct control, the United States practiced what might best be called the imperialism of interference in its relations with Latin America. This took various forms: periodic military intervention to impose regimes stamped with U.S. approval; corrupt manipulation or infiltration of elites; covert destabilization campaigns; coups and revolutions incited or suppressed, as convenient; aid packages tied with political strings; and usually, in the background, "business imperialism," pouring investment into the hemisphere and milking money out. Mexico, Panama, Nicaragua, Cuba, and Grenada were invaded— some of them repeatedly—not in response to any real threat to world peace but to preserve American interests or enforce U.S.–approved changes of government. Panama, indeed, was originally a creation of U.S. self-interest, hived off from Colombia to facilitate the construction of a canal under U.S. control. Coups d'état have been engineered in many other countries, and revolutions have been launched with U.S. connivance, as Uncle Sam "cut switches for bad boys."

Sometimes U.S. anxiety was excited by genuinely American threats: by cross-border "banditry" during the Mexican Revolution; by fascist and "fascisizing" movements in the thirties and forties; by the competition of pirate products and cheap labor at intervals throughout the century; by Communist insurgency and "urban guerrilla" movements that became a focus of fear in the 1960s; by the Colombian drug trade toward the end of the century; by illegal immigration. Usually, however, Latin America lacked the power to menace her northern neighbors with anything homegrown. For most of the first half of the century

U.S. policy was chiefly concerned with outstripping or excluding European rivals for trade and military-training contracts—mostly British, German, French, and, by the 1930s, Italian, for Mussolini invested heavily in buying up Latin American fascists.

This was a continuation of long-standing U.S. policy: the Monroe Doctrine, which by the early twentieth century had come to mean, shorn of rhetoric, that the United States would tolerate in the Americas no imperialism but its own. Whether it was British monopolists trying to control Latin America's economic infrastructures, European belligerents targeting Latin America's wealth in strategic raw materials, or Nazi "boys from Brazil" plotting secessionist "Aryan" states, all forms of European cupidity seemed hostile. Before the First World War, Latin America was a battleground of business imperialism. Britain started with an advantage. She funded two thirds of the foreign investment in the continent. She controlled over half the tonnage of Argentine and Brazilian ports. Railways, which linked the ports to the centers of production, were, over much of the continent, a British preserve; the railways of Brazil and Argentina were almost wholly British-owned. Weetman Pearson, the British M.P., was lampooned as "the member for Mexico" because of the scale of his interests in that country. Elevated to the peerage in 1910, he emblazoned his coat of arms with the image of a Mexican peon; allegedly, he looted more from Mexico than any man since Cortés. When Hugh Pollard went to Mexico as a young engineer in 1910, he found a country where "everybody has something in the way of a concession and only needs a little capital to become a millionaire."

Pollard argued that Mexico's best destiny lay through incorporation into the British empire. Reluctantly, however, he conceded that it was already too late. The Yankees were taking over. Since the Mexican War, they had grabbed half of Mexico's national territory, and now they were buying up as much as they could of the rest. José Posada agreed. In *Las bicicletas* of 1913, he depicted gringo imperialists as modern versions of the horsemen of the apocalypse, along with fraudsters, corrupt politicos, syphilitic prostitutes, and "bad Mexicans who help the foreigners." Deepening U.S. involvement in Mexico was part of a continent-wide phenomenon. Between the beginning of the twentieth century and the outbreak of the First World War, U.S. investment in Latin America more than trebled. Britain was still dominant, holding more than half the region's foreign debt, but the United States moved into second place, eclipsing the Germans and greatly exceeding the French.

The World Wars, both of which impoverished Europe and enriched America, subverted the Europeans' power and brought their efforts to an end. There was a brief period of quiescence in the late 1940s, when the United States felt unthreatened in its own hemisphere and largely withdrew from active engagement in neighbors' affairs, setting up instead the Organization of American States. The United States' plan was to make this a strategic security organization. It became a notorious "talk shop."

For most of the next two generations, however, there was a new enemy: "international communism," or Soviet policy, which seemed always to be seeking fiefs in the Americas. The United States' attitude toward Latin America seemed to mimic Russia's in Eastern Europe: here was space for "satellites" whose freedom to trade in strategic materials or make military alliances would be circumscribed by collective and bilateral treaties. John Foster Dulles, the "cold warrior" who shaped U.S. foreign policy during the Eisenhower years, was obsessed by the fear that "he would wake up one morning and read in the newspapers that there had happened in South America the same kind of thing as happened in China in 1949." The danger arose—at least in northern perceptions—when a moderate left-wing government in Guatemala declined to restore nationalized assets to the gigantic U.S. multinational corporation, the United Fruit Company. In 1954 the CIA organized a coup and supplied weapons to its creatures. Guatemala became a tame dependency, but the results were morally woeful: the extinction of democracy, the perpetuation of nasty right-wing dictatorships, the incubation of nasty left-wing guerrillas. It became a common pattern for victim states of gringo paternalism. It made the United States unpopular in its "backyard." In 1958, when U.S. vice president Richard M. Nixon, who made himself the voice of anticommunism, visited Lima, his bodyguards drew their guns to protect him from the resentment of the crowds in the streets.

Cuba complicated matters. Here, in 1959, the guerrillas were successful in taking over the state. Every backhanded U.S. attempt to destabilize socialism and engineer invasions failed. The intruded leader, Fidel Castro, was a natural showman with an austerely utopian vision for his country. He had flirted with the American dream in his youth, longing to play baseball for the Yankees, and thought Cuba Libre could really be procured by mixing rum with Coca-Cola—harnessing American aid for egalitarianism. But U.S. indifference to Cuba's misgoverment, which left the countryside to the caciques and the streets to the gangsters, turned him toward socialist "solutions." He crafted Cuba into a "model of socialism," which he exhibited to the world and recommended widely—to Africa and Latin

America in particular. He fomented other republics' guerrilla movements. In 1962 he permitted Russian bases to be built on Cuba, genuinely threatening to alter the equilibrium of world power by bringing the whole of the United States within striking distance of Russia's potential nuclear task force. U.S. president John F. Kennedy foundered into crisis, inaugurating an unsustainable blockade. Luckily for him, the Russians—*"maricones sin cojones,"* Castro complained—handed him a triumph by effectively conceding the Americas as a zone of U.S. influence in exchange for the withdrawal of U.S. missiles from Turkey. Castro's fangs were drawn, though he continued to snap at the United States with toothless mordancy. He remained immovable and irremovable, a permanent embarrassment and reminder of U.S. failure.

Because of Cuba, every other potential Communist "domino" on the American board became a major issue for U.S. policy for the rest of the cold war. In 1964 a U.S.–inspired coup felled a reformist Bolivian government that had dared to nationalize the tin mines. In the Dominican Republic in 1965, twenty thousand U.S. troops invaded to frustrate a supposed "second Castro." The United States funded the conspiracies that overthrew elected left-wingers João Goulart in Brazil and Salvador Allende in Chile. After a flirtation that seemed to be working, the Reagan administration turned on the idiosyncratic Sandinista regime in Nicaragua in the eighties; the Sandinistas then demonstrated their democratic credibility by accepting electoral defeat. Meanwhile, American invaders had suppressed "the People's Republic of Grenada." U.S. credentials as the champion of democracy and guardian of human rights were besmirched by subsidies for right-wing regimes and subversion of those of the left. The interventionist habit died hard. Even in 2001 the CIA was implicated in a failed attempt to oust the left-wing Venezuelan regime of Hugo Chávez. By then, however, the hallmark anxieties of U.S. policy in Latin America had shifted. In the final decade of the twentieth century, when the Communist threat had collapsed and the Soviet Union dissolved, the United States remained entangled in the politics of the hemisphere, but now with a different agenda: trying to fit Latin America into the "New World Order" by stabilizing democracy; fighting a "war on drugs" by stamping on the narcotics "barons" and targeting their political allies. Indeed, the arrival of the "New World Order," which required the United States' services as a global policeman, imposed or encouraged further interventions and seemed to herald a new period of ever more widespread and intrusive American interventions.

FROM POSTIMPERIALISM TO COUNTERCOLONIZATION

A curious—to me, the most curious—feature of this long history of U.S. imperialism and quasi imperialism in the Americas is that it went on for so long during a period when the role of the United States in the world was that of an anti-imperialist crusader. The country's self-appointment to this role is one of the most remarkable, albeit least investigated, transformations in American history. It occurred with relative suddenness sometime between intervention in the Mexican Revolution, an adventure that lasted into early 1917, and America's entry into the First

World War that April, which was proclaimed by President Wilson with non-imperial and even anti-imperial reasons. America's last act of territorial aggrandizement—the effectively forced purchase of the Virgin Islands—was completed in the same year. There has surely never been a power in history that has won so many wars and acquired, in consequence, so little territory or exacted so few reparations as the United States after 1917.

Numerous explanations have been adduced for the sudden self-transformation from imperial opportunist to anti-imperial propagandist. It owed something to the influence of Wilson's personal idealism, something to the circumstances of America's intervention in a European war, which had to be justified to the American electorate in terms calculated to appeal to the anti-imperialist majority and the millions of escapees from Old World empires. It owed, too, something to the failure of America's involvement in the Mexican imbroglio and something to the long-term effects of the work of anti-imperial intellectuals like Thoreau and Mark Twain, whose numbers had grown proportionately to America's share of the "white man's burden." Less convincingly, American anti-imperialism has been regarded as beyond need of explanation, part of an inherent tendency or pervasive tradition of American history, according to which democracy is necessarily anti-imperial.

Once America gave up imperialism, she stuck to the new program with extraordinary consistency. Having championed the principle of self-determination, she withdrew, during the 1920s and 1930s, from most of the territories she had occupied without consent. In 1934 the Indian Reorganization Act even selectively restored a measure of autonomy to some tribes. After the Second World War, in urging other colonial powers to forgo their empires, America was morally armed by her own fulfillment of a prewar promise to grant Filipino independence. Accusations of imperialism never really stuck when they were flung at the United States by cold-war Communists— despite the vast increase of America's informal power, the growth of the volume of debt she held, the number of international corporations she hosted, and the gradual worldwide take-up of technologies she developed.

Yet the Americas were an exception, as if exempted from a full measure of U.S. magnanimity: Uncle Sam's backyard still got swept out regularly. And the only overseas territories the United States failed to decolonize were Puerto Rico and the Virgin Islands. In Puerto Rico, imperialism remains an issue. The island remains a laboratory of "colonial experiment"—subject to unsuccessful Americanization, irked by mainland control over issues of environmental policy, fishing, and defense. Its long-term status is unresolved. It is an American anomaly, poised irresolubly between irreconcilable options: full independence or statehood within the United States; it is likely that, given the chance, most Puerto Ricans would accept statehood, unlikely that the U.S. Congress would concede it. The United States would probably grant independence if it were allowed to do so, but most Puerto Ricans are reluctant to endorse such a policy on the grounds that it would let the mainland redeem its responsibilities too cheaply.

Independence, if Puerto Rico had it, would not loosen the economic grip of the United States. Old-style dependency does not need to be clenched in formal power structures. The Dominican Republic and Jamaica resemble Puerto Rico; they are sources of cheap migrant labor for the States. Elsewhere, Americanization is the result of mimesis. Meanwhile, culture accompanies muscle. American popular culture, irresistible in the world, spills readily into the rest of the Americas. In one respect, Latin America gets a peculiar degree of attention; Protestant missions in Latin America have been inveterate exporters of U.S. culture, who threaten to call a Protestant New World into existence to redress the balance of a North America transformed by Catholic demographics.

For the vital counterpart of Americanization is "Latinization"—the "countercolonization" of the United States by migrants from the rest of the Americas, especially from Latin America and, above all, from Mexico. As the rest of the Americas gets more like the United States, so the United States gets more like the rest of the Americas. "Latinos" are now the biggest minority in the United States. Most are Spanish-speaking, Catholic, and of *indio* ancestry. This is genuinely a phenomenon of countercolonization, because the U.S. Southwest, where new migrants arrive, wetbacked from the Rio Grande or tumbled from the backs of trucks, was territory annexed by U.S. imperialism—"our land," says Carlos Fuentes, the Mexican intellectual. People overestimate the likely long-term effects of this migration. Unless Spanish-speaking organizations invest a lot more in Hispanophone education, publishing, and broadcasting, the United States is not going to become a Spanish-speaking or even a bilingual country. The growth in the numbers of Spanish speakers is a function of immigration, not of the durability of Spanish in the face of Anglophone prejudice. Families tend to lose touch with the language over two or three generations. Latinos are likely to end up like Italian Americans or Polish Americans—

minorities with selective, though substantial, cultural memories that do not include the use of their ancestral language. However, because of their numbers, the proximity of their ancestral homes, and the lateness of their arrival, they will be a bridge to the rest of the Americas and a lobby for closer pancontinental collaboration.

FROM EMPIRE TO INFLUENCE

America's swing away from imperialism is best understood, I think, in the context of the sudden outburst of peacefully transmitted American influence in the world—and especially in Europe—in the 1890s and early 1900s. To appreciate its impact and novelty, we have to glance back over the relationship between Europe and America, one of relatively short duration in world-history terms. Of course, as we have seen, America continuously exerted varying degrees of influence on the Old World, from the sixteenth century onward: at first by way of the "Renaissance Discovery of Man" and the "Columbian Exchange" of biota. In the eighteenth century, American landscape, I believe, nourished early romantic sensibilities in Europe. The presumed noble savagery of some of its inhabitants had a corresponding effect, adding to the romantic image of the earth a romantic image of humankind, as well as encouraging Europeans to find wisdom in their own "common man" (see pages 79–80).

After the failure of the French Revolutionary experiment, however, no political, ideological, or cultural movement of American origin again had a significant impact on the Old World for about a hundred years. Individual artists and writers of American provenance were recognized in

Europe, but no homegrown American culture took root in the Old World—unless one counts spiritualism, which originated around a middle-class dining table in upstate New York in 1842 and within a couple of generations approached the proportions of a mass religion on both sides of the Atlantic. In a world like ours—thoroughly steeped in American influence—this is a problematic matter, hard to grasp, harder to explain.

Even democracy, in the Old World, was more admired than imitated and more feared than admired. In the early nineteenth century, democracy seemed to be one of the "peculiar institutions" of the United States, mistrusted by most Europeans. But American evidence was intruding into the way the Old World thought about politics. Tocqueville systematically introduced American democracy to the world. *Democracy in America* remains one of the most influential books about the United States because of the way its appeal straddles political chasms. His recommendations made him a hero of constitutionalists and liberals. His aristocratic sangfroid in the face of popular sovereignty helped reconcile reactionaries to peaceful change. His prescriptions ultimately triumphed. Democracy became the first American cultural product to conquer the Old World, even before cheap music, casual manners, and fast food.

This consummation, however, was long delayed, while reactionary statesmen did a good job of propping up "moldering edifices" and the American Civil War discouraged imitators. When European constitutions began to make real progress toward democracy in the last years of the nineteenth century, the blueprint owed most to the publication in 1888 of a guide to the "American commonwealth" by Oxford historian and professor of jurisprudence James

Bryce, who had been to America three times on what would now be called "fact-finding" missions. He drew up an extraordinary "shopping list" of lessons that European polities could learn from America. Manhood suffrage, for instance, needed to be tempered by property qualifications, since in Bryce's opinion, for blacks and the poor "a vote is a means of mischief." Salaried politicians were to be avoided; they tended to mercenary motives, venal habits, and, in the context of a strong party system like that of the United States, irrational partisanship. Plebiscites were a good idea, but an elected judiciary was not. Separation of church and state was advisable. Sagaciously, Bryce warned that democracy tended to make politics unattractive to the best men and detected in America "a strong plutocratic element . . . and the fact that it is entirely unrecognised . . . makes it not less potent, and possibly more mischievous." On the whole, however, despite many exclusions, the general trend of American political development, he found, was exemplary or at least ineluctable. Bryce likened it to "Dante's lamp, whose light helps those who come after it."

In parallel with the promotion of democracy, the United States became identified with the notion of "the rights of man." The U.S. Declaration of Independence identified the key rights as "life, liberty and the pursuit of happiness." The first was ignored by all states, which continued to put people to death when it suited them. The second and third seemed, at first, too vague to change the course of history; they could be ignored on the specious grounds that different people had conflicting claims to liberty and happiness. In Latin America, variant versions of the U.S. Declaration's list became fossilized in all the republics' constitutions. In France, echoed in the revolution, they were repeatedly sidelined by illiberal governments. Even in America, the founding Declaration's supposed "human rights" were long denied to slaves and their black descendants. But the idea acted on the world in an unexpected way. In the late nineteenth and twentieth centuries, it became the basis of the "American dream," according to which everyone in America could pursue a kind of happiness—material prosperity—with encouragement from the state, instead of the usual interference. In partial consequence, the United States became the richest and therefore the most powerful country. By the turn of the millennium, the American example was a magnet for the world. Most countries copied the institutions—a free market, a democratic constitution, and the rule of law—that made the American dream deliverable.

In the same period, wide international agreement—to which most states signed up, with varying degrees of sincerity and commitment, in the Helsinki Process of 1975–1983—defined more human rights: of immunity from arbitrary arrest, torture, and expropriation; of family integrity; of peaceful association for cultural, religious, and economic purposes; of participation in politics, with a right of self-expression within limits required by public order; of immunity from persecution on grounds of race, sex, creed, sickness, or disability; of education; and of a basic level of shelter, health, and subsistence. Life and liberty, however, remained problematic: life, because of abiding disputes over whether the right applies to criminals, the unborn, and euthanasia victims; liberty, because of disparities of power. These continued to leave many people effectively defenseless against predatory states, criminal organizations, and rich corporations. In the early twenty-first century, the rhetoric of human rights has triumphed almost everywhere, but the full reality has yet to reach most of the world.

For most of the intervening period, America influenced Europe by reflecting back at her ideas of European origin, while nothing peculiarly American captured European imaginations in the realms of high culture and thought. In the last decade of the nineteenth century, however, American cultural influence suddenly began to radiate. The first world-conquering American culture was musical. In 1893 and 1894, in his *New World* Symphony and his "Biblical Songs," Dvořák, who had spent some years running an American conservatory, helped alert the world to the music of Negro spirituals. The first distinctive American art form to have a transforming effect on the Old World was ragtime. Debussy wrote "The Golliwog's Cakewalk" between 1906 and 1908, and within a decade or so ragtime rhythms had intruded into work by Satie, Hindemith, Stravinsky, and the young Darius Milhaud. The plaudit "*Ausgezeichnet ist Rag-time* [ragtime is excellent]," was ascribed to Kaiser Wilhelm II in alleged response to a performance by some of John Philip Sousa's bandsmen on one of their European tours. Puccini wrote what he thought was Zuni music into his 1910 work for New York's Metropolitan Opera, *La fanciulla del West*. American musical taste went on to invade Europe on a vast scale as a result of the First World War, with the victories of jazz, the conquests of American musical comedy in European theaters, and sallies from Tin Pan Alley and Hollywood; the songs marched with the troops. Puccini's heroine Magda, in 1917's *La rondine*, sings of love in ragtime. Rag had predisposed Europe to look to America for innovative music and good tunes.

Meanwhile, American visual art, it is often claimed, remained dependent on European inspiration until well into the second half of the twentieth century. This, however, overlooks two facts: first, the importance of architecture, which is the only genuinely popular kind of high art because people who never go to galleries cannot help but see it on their way to work. In the ragtime years, American architecture was taking a new departure, typified by the work of Frank Lloyd Wright and Louis Sullivan, for whom architecture was "but a part of democracy." Wright's *Collected Works* were published in Germany in 1910 to enormous éclat. The steel-framed skyscraper, invented in Chicago in the 1880s, became a conspicuously distinctive American gift to the world. When the Woolworth Building was completed just before the First World War, it was the most eye-catching edifice in the world, the most ambitious, perhaps, since the pyramid of Cheops. Though it was a while before Europeans imitated them, skyscrapers "intrigued the European public" and inspired "romance and fantasy."

In any case, the most pervasive of American visual arts is film, followed by television and advertisers' graphics. The U.S. film industry leapt to maturity during the First World War, the era of D. W. Griffiths's liberal-humanist epics *Intolerance* and *The Birth of a Nation,* as well as Thomas Ince's pacifist tableau, *Civilization.* Hollywood cannot be said to have sustained the moral high seriousness of those years, but its influence grew as ever more moviemaking talent got concentrated in the big-budget, studio-strewn suburb. By the 1930s movies were easy to show and easy to see in most of the world. Where there were no cinemas, there were itinerant projectionists. Film became the art most people saw most of. Hollywood not only filled late-twentieth-century minds with images of directors' choosing and scattered role models across the globe; it also projected America's version of itself.

While American art and music attained a new impact beyond America, so did American thought and science. In 1907, William James published *Pragmatism,* which sold sixty thousand copies in Europe. It was a truly homespun American philosophy, drafted for America by a thinker who resented his brother's notorious self-Europeanization and who crafted a thought system syncopated to the hustle of American life and the bustle of American business. In science, by the beginning of the twentieth century, America already had a reputation for inventing world-changing technology: the telegraph, the safety elevator, the telephone, the mimeograph, the sound recorder. The Saint Louis World's Fair of 1904 was, in some respects, a showcase for American technical inventiveness. The Wright brothers, meanwhile, enhanced this reputation by beating the rest of the world to the creation of a viable manned flying machine. At about the same time, American methods were launching a scientific revolution in the field of anthropology. Among the supposedly scientific certainties treasured in the late-nineteenth-century West was that of the superior evolutionary status of some peoples and some societies: an image of the world sliced and stacked in order of race. It was upset thanks largely to an undersung hero of the Western liberal tradition: Franz Boas exploded the fallacies of racist craniology and outlawed the notion that societies could be ranked in terms of a developmental model of thought.

The cultural influence of Latin America outside the hemisphere was limited to two realms: popular music and serious creative literature. Finns will tell you the tango is their national dance. "Latin American" is a dance-band style vaguely recognizable as genuinely Latin American in origin. Hollywood helped popularize the music of the mariachi and the marimba. Carmen Miranda made the rumba and the samba sexy. When I was little, Paraguayan *conjuntos* interpreted traditional Latin American music to the world and made cover versions of the embarrassingly awful repertoire of midcentury crooners to the twang of the *arpa india*. Since then, the music of various Latin American countries has had spasms of intercontinental popularity—the Brazil of the bossa nova, the Cuba of the Buena Vista Social Club, the Dominican Republic of the merengue. In recent years, however, "Latin" has been replaced by "Latino": the big music industry in the United States and the big opportunities for Hispanic performers to reach a vast public start on North American platforms.

Poetry and the novel, meanwhile, have remained a genuine preserve of Latin American excellence; thanks to the size of the market and the integrity of intellectual values in the Spanish-speaking world, writers of serious fiction have been appreciated at home in Latin America and so have sometimes been able to command attention abroad. In the late twentieth century magical realism became a worldwide fashion in fiction. The enmity of Mario Vargas Llosa and Gabriel García Márquez can generate column inches in celebrity-gossip glossies. The honor roll of novelists may be the only list of global greatness in which Argentina is disproportionately well represented. Nicaragua has fewer world-famous artists than Belgium, but it does have Rubén Darío. Pablo Neruda has featured as a protagonist in a popular movie.

AMERICAN ALSO-RANS

Such exceptions apart, the Americas outside the United States have been twentieth-century also-rans. The other countries of the hemisphere participated in the global rise of American culture mainly as recipients of the influence and, at times, the orders of the United States. They sometimes practiced resistance or affected indifference but always with unfortunate effects. The shame of the development gap became a feature of collective psychology. Self-measurement against the United States was a constant call to experiment and a perpetual source of frustration.

Argentina might have been the United States or, at least, the Canada of the south. A great future was repeatedly predicted for the country from the mid–nineteenth century onward, as the United States demonstrated the ways of greatness: unification by railroad, domestication of the grassland, extirpation of native peoples, selective industrialization, mass immigration. Between 1857 and 1930 Argentina made a net gain of three and a half million migrants. Immigration supplied 60 percent of the total population increase. By 1914, when 13 percent of the U.S. population was foreign-born, the corresponding figure in Argentina was 30 percent. In the early twentieth century, with almost the world's highest rates of increase in population and production, Argentina swelled in confidence. The cocksure swagger for which the country became notorious was expressed in an oath of allegiance introduced for schoolchildren in 1909; it proclaimed Argentina "the finest country on earth." With "blind faith in their glorious destiny," Argentinians believed they "would know no history without triumph."

Disillusion is optimism's usual reward. Ortega y Gasset saw it coming in the 1920s: "The promises of the pampa, so generous, so spontaneous, go so often unfulfilled. . . . Defeats in America must surely be worse than elsewhere. A man is suddenly mutilated, left high and dry, with no treatment for his wounds." By 1935, Argentina's own Manuel Gálvez concluded that in creating the country, "God made a mistake." Loneliness became the leitmotiv of literature in a land that the cartography of the time left tapering off the end of the world. "Europeans," pleaded Carlos Galvez in 1937, "can hardly imagine how tragic is our loneliness."

Yet the real problem was the nature of Argentina's immersion in the world economy. Primary-producing and export-led, Argentina's economy was a barometer of the world's economic weather. The country plunged with every downturn. Tango lyrics of the thirties agonized over the effects of the slump; in words sung by the barroom idol Discepolín, ironic paeans to filth and money resound: "Jesus was worth the same as the thief." Celedonio Flores sang of "the anger of men who are strong but . . . helpless in the face of hunger." Argentina responded by trying to escape the primary-product trap by hectic industrialization. The number of workers employed in industry more than doubled in a decade. By 1943, industry had taken over from agriculture as the biggest sector. But the war crippled Argentina's main trading partner, Britain. After it, Argentine meat fed impoverished ex-belligerents on credit. In 1948 the United States decreed that Marshall aid could not be used to buy Argentine produce. Meanwhile, the new industrial workforce literally ate into exportable resources. The export-substitution policies of the charismatic demagogue Juan Perón succeeded in reducing trade and impoverishing the workforce. He was a mountebank dictator splattered with motley: the shameless personality cult of his wife—"the martyr of the shirtless"—and the vacuous pseudoideology of "justicialism," which mixed fascist and social-Catholic rhetoric.

Every new effort of the second half of the twentieth century ended up grounded. Economic failure repeatedly arrested democratization as emergency conditions made men surrender to quick-fix dictatorships. The last short-lived miracle, contrived in the 1990s by pegging the peso to the U.S. dollar, is ending in austerity, tears, and threatened political turbulence as I write these lines in the closing days of 2001; the modest world economic downturn of the new millennium, which most economies survived—including some of the reputedly most fragile in the world—proved intolerable to Argentina. Today's newspaper carries stories about Spanish immigrants abandoning Argentina to go back home and of the popularity of a new board game called Deuda Eterna, the object of which is to "defeat the I.M.F." The search for explanations of failure has become a national pastime.

Neocolonialism—first of Britain, then of the United States—has been a favorite culprit. Self-critical Argentines—their numbers grow as crises multiply—have cursed their Spanish and Indian genes: gaucho machismo, Hispanic anarchy. Or they have repudiated "racial degeneracy" brought by the immigrants, or the complacency induced by promise, where "personal sacrifice and responsibility" seemed unnecessary. Foreigners have even blamed "something in the soil" or the national character. Ortega found Argentinians typified by gargantuan appetites, indiscipline, narcissism, and incompetence. The explanations all have something in common: they represent failure as a scourge of God, the outcome of moral defects. This is dangerous. It distracts attention from adjustable problems of politics and economics and starts self-fulfilling prophecies of doom. In Argentina, intellectual apprehension of failure preceded the event. It is a classic case of a country that has talked itself into decline.

Argentina is not the hemisphere's only case of unbearably great expectations. Frustration is the American disease par excellence. The examples of the countries that have escaped it only make its effects on the sufferers more acute. Chilean historiography has its own exceptionalist tradition. The country's independence movement was driven by the conviction—still unrealized—that Chile could be "the emporium of the earth." In the nineteenth century, Chileans, invincible in their wars against Peru, dreamed of turning their country into "the England of the Pacific." They became in their own estimation the "model republic," albeit not without self-criticism; "Everyone," announced a newspaper in 1858, "is shouting that Chile is the model republic of South America. What on earth can the others be like?" If these dreams never came true, if the expectations could not be sustained, it was perhaps because of the stagnancy of an economy repeatedly arrested in attempts at diversification. For most of the independence era, Chile was a victim of her own bonanzas—first copper, then nitrates—which kept her reliant on single products; then, in the second half of the twentieth century, fledgling industrialization was overshadowed by ideological squabbles between seekers of rival "Chilean paths" to socialism or "liberal revolution." Only in the last decade of the century did genuine economic pragmatism prevail.

Uruguay, "the Switzerland of America," has perhaps the best twentieth-century record south of Costa Rica, more progressive than Switzerland, for most of the twentieth century, in women's rights, labor laws, welfare provision, and economic regulation. Democracy lasted, with intervals, for about two thirds of the last century, a durability more impressive than most European countries could manage. Some of the social and political features that commonly accompany democracy—urbanization, literacy, relatively high and relatively well distributed wealth—were characteristic of Uruguay in the same period. But the electoral system, for most of the time, was highly idiosyncratic; the man with the most votes did not necessarily become president unless his party as a whole also outscored its rivals in a simultaneous election. This unstable system subverted successful candidates' legitimacy and encouraged "unholy alliances" contrived to provide electable slates, not workable governments. In the 1960s the Tupamaros guerrillas established a reputation in the shanties and tenements as "a big band of people who want equality and justice for everybody." Uruguay submitted, like the rest of the South American "cone," to military rule in the early 1970s, although—remarkably—after a few years of repression, the miltary accepted an unrigged plebiscite for the restoration of democracy in 1980.

Mexico, too, seems condemned to be "always a bridesmaid" of perpetual potential. Its twentieth century began well. The long-standing dictator, Porfirio Díaz, shared the virtue ascribed by a courtier to Louis XI of France, who "oppressed his people himself but would allow no one else to do so." But he became a victim of his success; as the economy grew, aspirations were aroused—among the excluded poor and peons as well as among the new liberal bourgeoisie. Economic promise was sacrificed in a revolution *"né de la prospérité"* that began in 1911, when the rural masses intervened in what at first seemed a power struggle inside the elite. There were only brief intervals in the ensuing chaos until the 1930s, but economic freedom was among the advantages sacrificed for political stability; private enterprise was plundered. Mexican governments were corporatist in inclination, rabidly anticlerical, economically defensive, and rhetorically antigringo. That phase lasted only until oil was nationalized in 1938. Under the shadow of the Second World War, Mexico became the "good neighbor" of the United States and switched to a strategy of halfhearted capitalism to restore the economy. This policy, patchily sustained, worked patchily. Economic growth kicked in. Foreign investment returned. In the 1960s a solution emerged to the apparently uncontainable population explosion: new strains of wonder wheat, developed in the United States using Mexican native varieties. But the glaring wealth gaps worsened. Ill-planned development spawned modern Mexico City, one of the world's most infernal wens, with a population (at its height in the 1990s) of about twenty million, inadequate housing, selective sanitation, and a permanent pall of atmospheric pollution.

Brazil has a similar history of "jam tomorrow." The Americas' "other giant" is almost as big as the United States and, by most standards of measurement, better endowed with natural resources. It is even, in some ways, more privileged in politics, since the unity of the country has never been seriously threatened, the mélange of races and cultures has coexisted without any violent outbreaks of ill feeling in modern times, and the many changes of regime have contained revolution, rather than following it or promoting it. Brazil is, in a sense, the China of South America—the most successful state in assimilating subject communities, the great instance of continuity in practice. Yet in comparison with the United States, it seems a giant with poor articulation and lumbering gait. Since Pedro Cabral's arrival, according to a leading Brazilianist, "Brazil has been seen as the land of opportunity, yet the effort by Brazilians to seize that opportunity has often fallen short." Most of Latin America is vulnerable to a similar kind of disillusionment. As Claudio Véliz has written, "The waning of the economic prosperity of Latin America during these closing decades of the century has been additionally disappointing because it contrasts so starkly with its earlier promise."

In the search for equality with the northern states, the rest of the Americas has tried many nostrums: various kinds of corporatism, socialism, anarcho-syndicalism, peasant romanticism, romantic indigenism. On the whole, however, the most obvious course has commended itself: If you can't beat them, imitate them. In the last twenty years of the twentieth century, faith in Chicago economics and the "End of History" has conquered almost the entire hemisphere. According to theory, economic freedom should bring political liberty. Modernization should promote democracy. Embourgeoisement should make all societies alike. It does not always happen like that. Economic liberalization, enforced by callous political repression, worked in the Chile of General Pinochet; the ultimate outcome was a democracy that now looks stable. This model has not proved itself more widely; in Argentina and Brazil in the 1960s and 1970s, the bourgeoisie, enriched by modernization, preferred to safeguard it by backing authoritarian politics. In both countries democratic systems were eventually reintroduced— thus far their courses resembled Chile's—but the economic dividends were shaky. Argentina has resumed her normal place in history: shattered hopes, frustrated expectations. Latin American stock market unit trusts, after a brief period of fashionability, have sunk into the *néant*. Meanwhile, the alternative strategy, conceived in revulsion from dependency, has not made Cuba more democratic or richer than her neighbors. Now that democratic capitalism has spread and more or less taken hold throughout the Americas—even Cuba has begun to soften—the rehomogenization of the hemisphere seems possible.

RETROSPECT AND PROSPECTS: GRINGOS AND GO-GETTERS

Stories help explain themselves; if you know how something happened, you begin to see why it happened. The reasons why North America rose to its present dominance in the hemisphere gain clarity with context. The transition was a relatively brief one and can be dated with fair exactness to the late eighteenth and early nineteenth centuries. How far back into a remoter past can it be traced? Is North American supremacy rooted in something deeper than the historical topsoil—in the nature of American societies, cultures, environments?

On the whole, it is a mistake to suppose that great events must have great causes or long-drawn-out origins. And sociocultural explanations of historical change, though beloved of scholars, are usually unsatisfactory, because no society or culture is fixed and unfluctuating; their transformations demand explanation in their turn. A modern trend is to whittle to fragments the vast schemes of causation historians formerly favored. Links are struck out of the *longue durée*. To understand the fall of Rome we do not need to go back to Augustus or even the Antoninuses. According to current scholarship, the Reformation happened because of the way things were in the sixteenth century, not the way they had been in the Middle Ages. British democracy is no longer thought to have started in the Germanic woods or "English individualism" among the Anglo-Saxons.

Similarly, it seems to me pointless to seek the origins of the rise of North America in a period when North America did not rise, or to search for causes in another continent—attributing Latin American retardation, for example, to a supposed "Iberian" curse, or the continent's present arrest to an enervating "legacy" in the remote past of a distant peninsula. Still, if we are to understand the present and future of the Americas, we need to be sure that we have not discounted possible explanations of their past without due consideration. So it is worth taking a moment to turn over the dust of traditional controversy on these matters and expose the bones of the unconvincing arguments: they concern, in turn, religion, culture, character, mind-set, and climate.

THE REWARD OF THE PHARISEES

As success gaps gape, it is easy to feel tempted by what I call the Pharisaic theory of history: material success is the reward of virtue. According to this argument, if people toward the northern end of the hemisphere have done better than the rest, it must be because they deserved to. Superior morals or superior culture or superior race destined them for superior performance. Although this theory is false, it has to be acknowledged that its advocates had good reasons for believing it. For much of the nineteenth century, American history seemed reflected in an Atlantic mirror. For Europe, too, was divided by a gap in registered success between north and south. "Nordics"—in a racial classification popular at the time—outstripped "Latins"; or, in cultural terms, Protestants beat Catholics and "Anglos" beat everyone else. So Britain became "the first industrial nation," "the workshop of the world," the heartland of liberty, the exemplar of political stability, and the metropolis of the world's mightiest empire. Meanwhile, the lands and cities of the Mediterranean—vital centers of bygone European civilization—were mired in stagnation or faltering in decline. Germany alone seemed to rival Britain for vitality. By transoceanic analogy, gringo victory at Cerro Gordo or Santiago de Cuba seemed like Prussian victory at Sedan: a halt on the march of the Saxon toward supremacy.

The losers always seemed to be Catholics, the winners Protestants. American Know-Nothings knew—or thought they knew—one big thing: Protestantism bred progress. The theory that Protestantism was an essential part of a sort of syndrome of cultural superiority became orthodoxy: Protestantism spawned capitalism and capitalism spawned imperialism. I am a Catholic, so I would like the theory to be true. It would comfort me to believe that capitalism and imperialism are peculiarly Protestant vices. Alas, they are prevalent among my coreligionists, too. Protestantism was of the essence of America, narrowly conceived in North American terms, because it nourished toleration, stimulated conflicts of conscience, and so led to concepts of civil liberty. Again the basic postulates were false. All religions favor toleration, except when they are in the ascendant. Puritan persecution of Catholics and of other Protestants was normal in early America. Quakers and Baptists, driven out of Massachusetts, founded their own states. Tolerant states were those where the founders' religion never established a firm ascendancy or where the need to promote colonization transcended confessional fastidiousness: Baptist Rhode Island, Catholic Maryland, Quaker Pennsylvania.

The dream or nightmare of a WASPish master race or supreme culture was illusory. "Anglo-Saxonism" crumbled when Britain and Germany fell out. No single race or single culture was responsible for the greatness of Britain or Germany or the United States; they were all successful in pluralism. Spasms of racism compromised or wrecked success. The British empire relied heavily on the collaboration of its own subject races and the manpower and brainpower of Celts, Catholics, and Jews—minorities who, because of underprivileged access to positions of power in the mother country, tended to be overrepresented in the British empire abroad. The United States has always been a tissue of minorities—and all the better for it. It was never more than a fantasy-Protestant land. Catholics participated at an early stage of the colonial era, especially in the making of Maryland. So did Jews. Quakers, who founded Pennsylvania and played a disproportionate role in the making of the country, are, at best, anomalous Protestants, because they value the teachings of the "indwelling spirit" above those of holy writ. According to historian John Bossy, an anthropologist from Mars would classify them with Catholics in a category apart from Protestants, properly so-called, whose distinctive characteristic is their Bible-based faith. Catholics have gradually played an ever bigger and more prominent role in the United States. The mythic importance of Protestantism in the United States resembles that of Calvinism in the Netherlands; it is the effect of an enchantment, unjustified by the numerical strength of the adherents of the religions concerned.

It is true that in the early years of the United States, Catholics were few, 35,000 out of 3.5 million in 1790. But the formative period from the mid–nineteenth century, when the West was won, was also the great era of Catholic increase, thanks first to the annexation of vast territories from Mexico, which boosted the numbers to 1.4 million out of 23 million in 1850. Reception of the "refuse" of Catholic Europe gradually led to the situation in America today, when Catholics are the biggest communion—as numerous as all the Protestants put together.

If the United States is not really Protestant, it must be questioned whether "Latin" America is really Catholic. Catholicism, as we have seen, has peculiar features in much of the New World. It enjoys constitutional privileges in many republics but has had to contend with fierce state secularism in Mexico and Cuba. All the Latin American republics have been dedicated to the Virgin under various advocations, and the abiding strength of the Catholic tradition to influence society has been visible in recent years—in, for example, the role played by the pope in resolving the Beagle Channel conflict, the spectacular political success of the Christian Democratic party in Chile, and the influence of liberation theology in such radical movements as those of the Sandinistas in Nicaragua and the Zapatistas in Chiapas. But, while the numbers of Catholics grow in North America, the numbers of Protestants grow in the South. There are now more Protestant pastors than Catholic priests in Brazil. A third of Guatemalans belong to Protestant sects, more than one in six of Chileans, Nicaraguans, and Costa Ricans. Evangelical movements, often backed by sects representative of the U.S. "moral majority," have been the fastest-growing fashions of the last fifty years in most of Latin America. They have exercised political influence in their turn, especially in Guatemala, where, under the crazed leadership of a self-proclaimed Evangelical, Efraín Rios Montt—or "Dios Montt," as satirists aptly called him—Protestant politics and a right-wing regime became effectively identical.

The assumption remains widespread that differences in political culture, broadly understood, correspond to differences in fortunes. Most of the Americas, thanks to historic legacies that go back at least to the Spanish and Portuguese empires—have a political culture dominated, it is said, by the "ethos of patrimonialism," whereas the United States was "born liberal." The Latin body politic is "organic" or "corporatist," whereas the United States is viscerally individualist, "the land of the free." Both moieties had Roman models, but the United States' was republican and the Latins' was imperial. This is one of Americans' fondest myths of themselves. I do not mean to suggest that they are not genuinely a free people who love liberty. Of course they are. Their faith in freedom is one of their touchingly—almost naïvely—endearing features, which makes foreigners like me feel happy and at home in the States. But that faith is not founded on individualism.

People in the United States are cloyingly gregarious, profoundly communitarian, boringly conformist. They get glutinously embedded in any community they can, outside their own families: the workplace, high school and college alumni associations, the neighborhood, the city, the church, the innumerable "membership associations" they all seem to belong to. Membership is treated as a religious obligation; it does not matter what you belong to as long as you belong to something. Some American sociologists seem seriously to think that it is better to belong to a hate group than to no group at all. Civic-mindedness, not individualism, is what makes "America" great. This is a truth about America so elusive that even Americans are, in general, unaware of it. American culture is not genuinely the product of rampant individualism but of historic values of solidarity. Mainstream America lives in small towns, where almost everyone knows almost everyone else, or neighborhoods where people feel they belong to one another. Civic commitment, which sacrifices spare time and reaches deep into pockets for the sake of collective projects, is far more impressive in America than in any other country known to me. Democratic decision-making touches levels unplumbed in Europe. Repugnance for class distinctions makes good manners easy to come by and bad manners undiscriminating in their effects. It was never self-help that made the United States great; it was mutual support. In the formative era of the modern American identity, for every gunslinger in the street or maverick in the corral, there were thousands of solid citizens in stockades and wagon trains.

Liberal democracy was not the only modern doctrine the United States exemplified for the world; it was also the home of early socialist experiments in collective utopianism. The frontier nurtured communitarianism; socialism throve in the soil of early America. Followers of Étienne Cabet, Robert Owen, and Charles Fourier constructed "backwoods utopias" on socialist principles: cities of Icarus that dared and failed. Today only their ruins remain; Karl Marx's prediction that America would be the first terrain of socialist revolution proved false, like most of his other predictions. But the desolate communes are a reminder of the evidence he had before him, and of how much America contributed to the development of socialism.

In any case, many of the political vices said to characterize Latin America—violence, anarchy, chaos irreparable except by military intervention—are more likely to issue from individualism than from corporatism. Because the same vices seemed apparent in Spain in the nineteenth century, it was convenient to blame the Spanish heritage. This cannot be right; areas of the Americas that Spain barely touched have been bogged down in underdevelopment and tortured by political instability. Revisions of nineteenth-century Spanish history have rehabilitated the economy; it was not underdeveloped by European standards or particularly backward in industrialization. The notion that Iberian political traditions were anti-individualist seems to have nothing to commend it except anti-Hispanic prejudice. It is part of the Black Legend. In reality, the histories of Spain and, to a lesser extent, Portugal have been characterized by individualist values. The word *liberal* in its political sense is one of the terms English owes to Spanish. Resistance to centralization has been fierce. Anarchism has been popular. There is a lot of truth in Salvador de Madariaga's old joke that democracy has historically been hard to sustain in Spain not because of a deficiency of individualism but because of a surfeit of it; to be truly representative, you would need thirty-five million political parties. Individualism is a universal trait. A scholar who scanned history for the origins of English individualism gave up the search; lost in the mists of time, it was to be found, he guessed, where English myth traditionally located it: in the Germanic woods. It is more likely that as a peculiarly English phenomenon it never really existed.

In history there is not, in my opinion, much difference between perception and reality. History offers few lessons. One of them, however, is that facts are less potent than the falsehoods that people believe. If enough people believe a falsehood, it eventually comes true; in the meantime, they behave as if it were true and its influence on the course of events becomes immense. It therefore matters little that the failure of most of the Americas has been misrepresented. The temptation to exaggerate the shortfall in success south of the Rio Grande has become virtually irresistible. Uruguay and Costa Rica, Venezuela and Colombia—the countries where democracy has been only occasionally interrupted, where civil conflicts have been merely sporadic rather than habitual, where external wars have been rare rather than regular, where economic disasters have been intermittent rather than routine—might be thought of as encouraging examples; instead, they get relegated to the class of "exceptions that prove the rule." And indeed, though they shine by comparison with their neighbors, they come off poorly when compared with Canada and the United States.

Perceptions are a function of perspective; shift perspective and you see things differently. If political stability is defined in terms of peaceful changes of government, Canada and the United States clearly have privileged histories; but if the durability of the political elite is the standard of measurement, then Brazil probably has the most remarkable record. It is a land of many coups but no revolutions. Still, it must be admitted that the usual rhythm of political life in the Americas, outside the United States and Canada, is hectic, with unpredictable syncopations. Where electoral processes are unreliable and routines irreproducible, violence interposes. Mexico had twenty presidents between 1840 and 1848. War made it an unusually intense period of political instability, even by Mexican standards, but this is another case where extremes are not unrepresentative. The longevity of some dictatorships made a telling contrast with habitual chaos. In 1911 the Mexican Revolution interrupted the thirty-five-year tenure of Porfirio Díaz; after ten years' bloody struggle for the control of central institutions, followed by a series of bloody rebellions—and, from 1926 to 1929, a serious, nationwide guerrilla war against clericalist resistance to an aggressively secular regime—the revolution brought stability of another kind—all too much of it for most tastes, since the same political party then remained in power for nearly seventy years from 1928 at the federal level and, for much of that time, manipulated the electoral system to keep power in the provinces.

If they are not matters of character, can the peculiar achievements of the United States and Canada be attributed to mental qualities—a distinctive "mind-set"? Again, this hardly seems worthy of serious consideration; it is obviously a partisan overgeneralization. Yet it remains a common opinion that Americans—the U.S. kind—are essentially "practical," whereas most other Americans are imaginative. South of the border, dreams take over from dollars, artists from craftsmen, creative minds from constructive ones. According to the brilliant formulation of Claudio Véliz, "Gothic foxes" outsmart "baroque hedgehogs." This is a Latin criticism and an Anglo-Saxon boast in a hemisphere of hustle and hassle, battle and bustle. "Getting things done" is a Yankee speciality; the Latins never get further than arguing and struggling about what those things should be.

Even if this line of argument were plausible, the facts belie it. It is true that the United States in modern times has registered exceptional levels of economic activity—by world standards, not just those of the Americas. But this is a function of superior opportunity—a large internal market, abundant cheap capital—rather than of magically transmutative effects of the United States on people who go to live there. In the era of ascent, the United States had a big single market: a population roughly equal to that of all the Latin American republics combined, in the mid–nineteenth century, with an urgent need to create their own wealth in the face of relatively modest natural resources. Yankees tired Dickens with telling him, "We are a trading people and we don't care for poetry." When Latin Americans have comparable opportunities and comparable needs, they produce comparable results. While still under Spanish rule, Cuba had the most precocious railway system in the Americas. Despite all the problems of the second half of the twentieth century, and the inglorious political record of most of that period, the Latin American regional economy grew fivefold.

For explaining American disparities, climatic theory is even sillier than the cultural theories. This has not inhibited some thinkers from espousing it. Hot tempers, hot peppers, and hot weather seem well matched. In an attempt to freeze out the stereotype, Chile has advertised its potential as a modern economy with the image of an iceberg. But there are too many climates in the Americas for climatic explanations to work. As we have seen, some climatic zones are common to North and South America, but they have nourished communities of unpredictably varying fortunes. The physical environment of the prairie resembles that of the pampa. Some parts of the Rockies resemble the Andes, others the Sierra Madre. The boreal and Antarctic cold zones have much in common. Virtually all habitable climates have been home to civilization; tropical rain forest, which is unrepresented in Canada and the United States, has produced some of the most spectacular. If anything, much of the territory of both those countries is extremely hostile to human settlement. This perhaps accounts for the relatively late start that advanced material civilization made in those parts of the Americas, compared with areas of civilizing precocity in Mesoamerica and the Andes. Insofar as climate is relevant, it makes the problem of the variety of experience more complex but does not help to solve it.

THE FUTURE

Initiative in the Americas is not about to return to Mexico or Peru. Nonnorthern Americas remain, in common perceptions, lands of political iniquities that seem unintelligible in English and so have come to be signified by unhappily naturalized words: *junta, pronunciamiento, cacique, guerrilla, cartel, caudillismo.* Economically, they are still regions of maddeningly unfulfilled promise. Most Americans outside the United States feel restive and frustrated at condemnation to *tercermundismo.* In a poll conducted in 1940, between a quarter and a half of U.S. respondents decribed the people of Central and South America as quick-tempered, emotional, backward, lazy, ignorant, suspicious, dirty, and proud. The only positive characteristics that attracted comparable levels of assent were "religious" (45 percent) and "friendly" (30 percent). Except inside Latin America, people forget to include the region in their lists of member states of "the West"; when Samuel Huntington wrote *The Clash of Civilizations* (1996), he did not know whether to include Latin America in Western civilization or not. In 2000 the economic thinker Juan Enríquez Cabot berated his fellow Latin Americans with their failures, generally expressed in terms of unfavorable comparisons with the United States. Only one, for instance, of the United States' top ten billionaires inherited his wealth; in Latin America, nine of the ten biggest personal fortunes were inherited. Ten of the top twelve U.S. companies were in the technology business; in Latin America, they were all in old-fashioned, labor-intensive industries supplying energy or manufactures. The United States' expenditure on technological R&D was 2.6 percent of GNP, Mexico's 0.3 percent. Peru registered no improvement in GDP per capita between 1970 and 2000. But the relationship between the United States and the rest of the hemisphere is likely to become less glaringly unequal in the foreseeable future.

For judging the performance of most American countries in the search for political and economic maturity, Canada makes a more realistic yardstick than the United States. It is too small, in terms of population, to rival the power of the United States or to resist its influence; but partly as a result of sheer contiguity, Canada has been able to share in its neighbor's success and achieve some comparable successes of her own in parallel. Despite a paucity of population, Canada has become home to one of the world's biggest economies. In the nineteenth century it became a state larger in territorial dimensions even than the United States and at the end of the millennium is, by the same measurement, easily the world's most extensive country. In the twentieth century Canada developed a reputation second to none in the hallmark virtues of a civil society: adherence to democracy, respect for human rights, accommodation of ethnic minorities, values of pluralism and multiculturalism imbedded in state institutions and laws, generous and efficient provision for social welfare, eschewal of militarism, and commitment to the pursuit of peace. Despite serious challenges to social peace in Canada over the century and a half or so of the state's existence, its political stability has exceeded even that of the United States. No revolution, no civil war, no uncontainable constitutional or ethnic conflict has ever seriously disturbed Canada's history or threatened resolution by serious violence; today, if Québec were to secede, Canadians would adjust unrancorously and devise some new form of association in which Québecois could be accommodated. Canada is close to being most people's ideal country, one of a handful where, according to soundings by pollsters, large numbers of people all over the world would like to live if they could.

Could the rest of the Americas perform a similar trick of self-transformation and catch up with the North? Some features of the current situation recall the historic conditions that made the North's leap forward possible. That leap coincided, if the account given above is right, with three vitally important circumstances: first, exceptionally favorable demographic changes; second, the availability—in the North American prairie—of a vast, previously underexploited environment and the means to transform it; and, finally, expanding economic opportunities created in part by a context of rapidly expanding trade and in part by the prospects opened up by the beginnings of the Industrial Revolution. In the eighteenth century the demographic problem that the North American colonies solved was shortage of population; in more recent times the problem in most of the Americas has been keeping population growth under control while maintaining a practical balance in the distribution of numbers between the generations. The signs are that this problem is now being solved naturally as Latin American birthrates decline to replacement levels. Over the next few decades there will be plenty of young people in the workforce, but the population will be stable, with a consequent easing of the strain on the economic infrastructure that has been so difficult to cope with in much of the region in the recent past.

Similarly, the great global growth of trade, from which the fledgling United States benefited, resembles the new commercial revolution of our times. Ever-freer trade, globalization, the worldwide near uniformity of liberal capitalism—these features of our time are riven with imperfections and unbalanced by inequalities, but they constitute a favorable background for growth in economies poised to take advantage. Liberal capitalism is not a magic formula for success, and the dollar is not magic money—Argentina found that out in the banking crash of 2001–2002. But immersion in ever-wider circles of economic cooperation—with their big markets and big pools of investment—does at last seem to be having a stabilizing effect on Latin America's national economies. The political dividend is obvious; not even the banking disaster could overturn Argentina's hard-won democracy. At present, for the first time in history, almost every state in the Americas has a stable political system favorable to economic freedom and to the exercise of commercial opportunities. At the same time, conditions of global competition are favorable for closer and more equal economic cooperation between the United States and the rest of the hemisphere. The opportunities are enhanced by the rapid development of new kinds of wealth creation. Most of the Americas missed out on the Industrial Revolution; the hemisphere-wide wealth gaps of the last two centuries have been among the consequences. Now postindustrial technology is exposing another vein of potential wealth; at present, North America is way ahead of the rest of the hemisphere in exploiting that potential, but it is probably not too late for Latin America to claim a fair share of the action. If, however, the new opportunities are left to the North, as industrialization was in the nineteenth century, it will not be surprising if the rest of the Americas remain mired in backwardness.

Finally, there are those underexploited environments to consider; the tropical forest, the ocean, and Antarctica could be to the twenty-first century what the prairies were to the nineteenth. While in Canada and the United States people were colonizing the prairies, scattering them with cities and making them erupt with industries, other American countries seemed only to scratch and scrape at their own wildernesses. The present dilemma is how to handle the new environmental temptations. We now have the technology to reap the ocean's bounty, farm the rain forest, make the ice bleed with minerals. Exploitation could mean obliteration—a transformation into unrecognizability, like the prairie beheld by Trollope (see page 139). Conservation could be expensive; if the world wants people in the Americas to preserve the rain forests and ice lands and seaworlds as wild gardens for the planet, we shall have to pay them to do so. The more likely outcome—a rational compromise, a program of planned exploitation—could help equalize the Americas and crown the reconvergence of historical trajectories in the hemisphere with justice.

BIBLIOGRAPHICAL ESSAY

This book is subtitled "A Hemispheric History" not because it is imperfectly rounded but because it is an attempt to cover the whole hemisphere. This has not been tried before, so there are no general works on the whole subject to rely on or recommend. What follows is an attempt to identify important texts on the topics I raise chapter by chapter, in the order in which they occur in this book. The results are bound to be selective, even among my own preferences and prejudices, and readers should be warned that any scholar's knowledge of the bibliography over the whole history of a hemisphere is bound to be patchy. I have tried to identify works or translations in English where they are known to me and, where appropriate, to point readers toward the most recent works I have encountered and the most useful bibliographical quarries.

CHAPTER 1: AMERICAS? AMERICA?

The pages on Vespucci by S. E. Morison in *The European Discovery of America: The Southern Voyages* (1974) have never been surpassed; to correct them and bring them up to date, consult the entry by me in *American Dictionary of Biography*, vol. 1 (1998). On the early cartography, the forthcoming *History of Cartography*, vol. 3, ed. D. Woodward, will supplant all previous work and will include extensive bibliographical information. On Columbus, see F. Fernández-Armesto, *Columbus* (1996), and W. D. and C. R. Phillips, *The Worlds of Christopher Columbus* (1992).

The eighteenth-century debate on American nature is surveyed by A. Gerbi, *The Dispute of the New World* (*La disputa del nuovo mondo*), and J. Canizares-Esguerra, *How to Write the History of the New World* (2000). The world picture of the colonial Maya is described in M. Restall, *The Maya World* (1997), and N. M. Farriss, *Maya Society Under Colonial Rule* (1984).

American utopianism would make a good subject for a comprehensive study. Meanwhile, on the sixteenth-century origins see J. Knapp, *An Empire Nowhere: England, America and Literature from Utopia to The Tempest* (1992); A. Milhou, *Colón y su mentalidad mesiánica en el ambiente franciscanista español* (1984); and G. Baudot, *Utopie et histoire au Mexique* (1977). The story of the next couple of centuries must be filled in with the help of work on millenarianism (see below). W. A. Hinds, *American Communities and Cooperative Colonies* (1908); C. Wittke, *We Who Built America* (1946); A. E. Bestor, *Backwoods Utopias: The Sectarian and Owenite Phases of Communitarian Socialism in America, 1663–1829* (1950); and D. D. Egbert, *Socialism and American Art* (1967), then take up the tale and make excellent guides to the radical religious and socialist utopias built in the United States in the last two or three centuries. My inclusion of Disneyland in the list of dream towns was inspired by an article by E. L. Doctorow reprinted in J. Carey, ed., *The Faber Book of Utopias* (1999).

The story told by Hugh Brody can be found in H. Brody, *The Other Side of Eden* (2000), which is an important chronicle of personal encounters with the peoples and environments of the American Arctic. A glaring example of Native American mythopoeia is V. Deloria, *Red Earth, White Lies* (1995).

The depiction of Ireland as American will be found in *Americana: The Americas in the World, Around 1850 (or "Seeing the Elephant" as the Theme for an Imaginary Western)* (2000), which is also a brilliant essay on American exceptionalism—a subject best explored with the help of B. E. Shafer, *Is America Different?* (1991); S. M. Lipset, *American Exceptionalism: A Double-Edged Sword* (1996); L. Harz and T. Wicker, *The Liberal Tradition in America* (1991); and C. Véliz, *The New World of the Gothic Fox* (1994). For exceptionalisms in Latin America, see, for instance, L. Whitehead, *Whatever Became of the Southern Cone Model?* (1982).

CHAPTER 2: BETWEEN COLONIZATIONS:
THE AMERICAS' FIRST "NORMALCY"

B. Trigger and W. E. Washburn, eds., *The Cambridge History of the Native Peoples of the Americas,* vol. 1: *North America* (1996), is a magisterial survey, uneven in places. It covers well the problem of the origins of the "first Americans," but this is a subject in flux, on which it is also helpful to read J. Adovasio, *The First Americans: In Pursuit of Archaeology's Greatest Mystery* (2002), an engaging, personal, partisan account that is up to date with the scholarship. Compare, however, the skeptical approach in F. Salomon and S. B. Schwartz, eds., *The Cambridge History of the Native Peoples of the Americas,* vol. 3: *South America* (1999). S. Krech, *The Ecological Indian* (1999), deals dispassionately with the Pleistocene extinctions and subjects many myths of later Native American history to searching examination.

On the origins and ecology of early food production, in the absence of a comprehensive study the best strategy is to piece together the facts from K. F. Kiple and K. C. Ornelas, eds., *The Cambridge World History of Food,* 2 vols. (2000).

Among the most useful studies of the early Andean civilizations, R. Burger, *Chavín and the Origins of Andean Civilization* (1995), and R. W. Keating, ed., *Peruvian Prehistory: An Overview of Inca and Pre-Inca Society* (1988), can be particularly recommended. On the Olmecs, I rely mainly on M. D. Coe et al., *The Olmec World: Ritual and Rulership* (1995), and E. P. Beson and B. de la Fuente, eds., *Olmec Art of Ancient Mexico* (1996). Revelatory on Teotihuacán is K. Berrin, ed., *Feathered Serpents and Flowering*

Trees: Reconstructing the Murals of Teotihuacán (1988). The best book on Tula is R. A. Diehl, *Tula: The Toltec Capital of Ancient Mexico* (1983). The Maya have been well served by writers of surveys. The best are N. Hammond, *The Maya* (1999), and M. D. Coe, *The Maya* (1990). On the writing system, Coe has also contributed the wonderful and inspiring *Breaking the Maya Code* (1992). The best edition and study of the Popol Vuh is Denis Tedlock, ed., *Popol Vuh: The Mayan Book of the Dawn of Life* (1985). On Mesoamerica generally, R.E.W. Adams and M. J. MacLeod, eds., *The Cambridge History of the Native Peoples of the Americas*, vol. 2: *Mesoamerica* (2000), is a valuable guide.

There is no scholarly consensus on the quipu, but C. Animato et al., eds., *Quipu: Il nodo parlante dei misteriosi Incas* (1989), is, right or wrong, a most exciting volume. Native maps in North America are comprehensively studied in J. B. Harley and D. Woodward, eds., *The History of Cartography*, vol. 2 (1988). On indigenous literature generally, the wonderful book by G. Brotherston, *The Book of the Fourth World* (1992), is unmissable.

My allusion on the Jornada de Muerte is to G. Pérez de Villagrá, *Historia de la Nueva Mexico, 1610,* ed. M. Encinias et al. (1992). An excellent short account of Chaco Canyon is in Trigger and Washburn, as above. See also S. Lekson et al., *Great Pueblo Architecture of Chaco Canyon* (1984). For Cahokia I rely chiefly on T. R. Pauketat and T. E. Emerson, *Cahokia: Domination and Ideology in the Mississippian World* (1997).

Iroquoian peoples are the subject of brilliant work by B. Trigger, *A History of the Huron,* 2 vols. (1996), and W. N. Fenton, *The False Faces of the Iroquois* (1987), as well as a useful short account by D. R. Snow, *The Iroquois* (1994).

There is now a fascinating exploration of the effects of El Niño in B. Fagan, *Floods, Famines and Emperors: El Niño and the Fate of Civilizations* (1999). For the Moche, who were perhaps its victims, see G. Bawden, *The Moche* (1996).

The Spanish sources I mention on the Amazon are collected in F. de Requena et al., *Ilustrados y bárbaros: Diario de la expedición de límites al Amazonas,* ed. M. Lucena Giraldo (1991), and G. de Carvajal et al., *La aventura del amazonas,* ed. R. Díaz (1986). The archaeological data are superbly surveyed in C. McEwan et al., eds., *Unknown Amazon: Culture and Nature in Ancient Brazil* (2001).

CHAPTER 3: COLONIAL AMERICAS: DIVERGENCE AND ITS LIMITS

On the colonial period, many scholars have been attracted to wide-ranging comparative studies of particular aspects of the history of the Americas; they are surveyed panoptically in a general comparative overview of the colonial Americas: J. E. Kicza, *Resilient Cultures* (2002). A brief and brilliant introduction to European overseas expansion as a whole is now available: D. Ringrose, *Expansion and Global Interaction, 1200–1700* (2000); D. W. Meinig, *The Shaping of America,* vol. 1: *Atlantic America, 1492–1800* (1986), is of great value and interest; P. Chaunu, *Conquête et exploitation des nouveaux mondes,* 2 vols. (1970), is the best available general history of European colonialism in the early modern period, with particular emphasis on the Americas.

L. Bethell, ed., *The Cambridge History of Latin America,* vols. 1 and 2 (1984), is the fullest survey of the Spanish and Portuguese colonies; A. Taylor, *American Colonies* (2001), does a similarly comprehensive job for North America; though occasionally old-fashioned, especially in its treatment of religion, this work is also remarkable for resisting myths of American exceptionalism and doing justice to many neglected themes. W. R. Louis, ed. in chief, *The Oxford History of the British Empire,* vol. 1, ed. N. P. Canny, and 2, ed. P. E. Marshall (1998), deal magisterially with the British colonies.

Colonial societies can be fully understood only from an indigenous perspective. Outstanding works written in this spirit include J. E. Kicza, ed., *The Indian in Latin American History* (2000); J. Lockhart, *The Nahuas After the Conquest* (1992); M. Restall, *Maya Conquistador* (1998); S. J. Stern and J. Axtell, *After Columbus: Essays in the Ethnohistory of Colonial North America* (1988); R. White, *The*

Middle Ground: Indians, Empires and Republics in the Great Lakes Region, 1650–1815 (1991); and E. Hinderaker, *Elusive Empires: Constructing Colonialism in the Ohio Valley, 1673–1800* (1997).

Study of the demographic collapse of the indigenous peoples has become bogged down in debate over irresoluble problems: How many natives were there? How many died? D. Henige, *Numbers from Nowhere* (1998), is partisan and rather intemperate but does demonstrate the difficulties brilliantly. N. D. Cook, *Conquest by Disease* (1998), is accessible, judicious, and up-to-date, though it treats the role of disease in "explaining" conquest with monocausal tenacity.

On "spiritual conquest" the agenda was set by R. Ricard, *The Spiritual Conquest of Mexico* (1967), written in rebuttal of secularist works by cultural anthropologists. It remains an invaluable work of reliable judgment. Innumerable studies have now made it clear that postconquest religion was a complex phenomenon that cannot be understood either merely as the triumphant outcome of "spiritual conquest" or as simply "syncretic." For exemplary studies, see K. Mills, *Idolatry and Its Enemies: Colonial Andean Religion and Extirpation, 1640–1750* (1997); S. MacCormack, *Religion in the Andes: Vision and Imagination in Early Colonial Peru* (1991); and W. B. Taylor, *Magistrates of the Sacred: Priests and Parishioners in Eighteenth-Century Mexico* (1996). For an exceptional case of Protestant missionary work, see N. Salisbury, "Red Puritans: The 'Praying Indians' of Massachusetts Bay and John Eliot," *William and Mary Quarterly,* 3rd s., 21 (1974), 27–54; for a general overview, C. Bernand and S. Gruzinski, *De l'idôlatrie: Une archéologie des sciences religieuses* (1988), can be heartily recommended. *Spiritual Encounters: Interaction Between Christianity and Native Religions in Colonial America* (1999), F. Cervantes and N. Griffiths, eds., provides an update on current trends in scholarship.

On religion in settler communities, J.C.D. Clark, *The Language of Liberty, 1660–1832* (1994), sees the American Revolution as a war of religion, in which connection see also E. T. Morgan, "The Puritan Ethic and the Coming of the American Revolution,"

William and Mary Quarterly, 3rd s., 25 (1967). P. U. Bonomi, *Under the Cope of Heaven: Religion, Society and Politics in Colonial America* (1986), is a traditional survey, F. Lambert, *Inventing the "Great Awakening"* (1999), a heterodox critique; both are outstanding. The study of settler religion in Catholic areas has focused on the clergy and the religious orders to the neglect of laypeople, but R. Greenleaf, *The Mexican Inquisition of the Sixteenth Century* (1969), is helpful. On millenarianism, see F. Graziano, *The Millennial New World* (1999), and R. H. Bloch, *Visionary Republic: Millennial Themes in American Thought, 1756–1800* (1985).

My account of slave religion in Brazil is largely based on W. Amado, ed., *A religião e o negro no Brasil* (1989); R. Bastide, *The African Religions of Brazil: Towards a Sociology of the Interpenetration of Civilizations* (1978); and A. Vogel et al., *A galinha-a'angola: Iniciacão e identidade na cultura afro-brasileira* (1993).

The best introduction to colonial slavery in general is J. Thornton, *Africa and the Africans in the Making of the Atlantic World* (1997). The most important studies include H. S. Klein, *African Slavery in Latin America and the Caribbean* (1986); K. F. Kiple, *The Caribbean Slave: A Biological History* (1984); P. D. Curtin, *The Rise and Fall of the Plantation Complex* (1990); and I. Berlin, *Many Thousands Gone: The First Two Centuries of Slavery in North America* (1998). On Brazil, A.J.R. Russell-Wood, *The Black Man in Slavery and Freedom in Colonial Brazil* (1982), should supplement the classic work of G. Freyre, *The Masters and the Slaves* (1946). W. D. Jordan, *White over Black: American Attitudes Toward the Negro, 1550–1812* (1977), deals with perceptions of slaves. On the slave trade, R. Blackburn, *The Making of New World Slavery: From the Baroque to the Modern, 1492–1800* (1996), and H. Thomas, *The Slave Trade: A History of the Atlantic Slave Trade, 1440–1870* (1997), are both gripping and instructive.

Maroons are a shamefully underresearched subject but can be approached with the help of B. Lamon Kopytoff, "The Early Political Development of Jamaican Maroon Societies," *William and Mary Quarterly*, 3rd s., 35 (1978), 287–307; R. Price, *Maroon Societies:*

Rebel Slave Communities in the Americas (1973); and D. Freitas, *Palmares: A guerra dos escravos* (1982). I must add, with thanks to Stuart Schwartz for the information, that this last work, though immeasurably interesting, contains many assertions that the archives do not seem to support.

For an introduction to the numbers, nature, and provenance of colonists, see I. Altman and J. Horn, *"To Make America": European Emigration in the Early Modern Period* (1991). The case of Virginia has inspired an enormous amount of superb scholarship, among which S. Morgan, *American Slavery, American Freedom: The Ordeal of Colonial Virginia* (1975); J. Horne, *Adapting to a New World: English Society in the XVIIth-Century Chesapeake* (1994); F. W. Gleach, *Powhatan's World and Colonial Virginia: A Conflict of Cultures* (1997); and T. W. Tate and D. L. Ammerman, eds., *The Chesapeake in the Seventeenth Century: Essays on Anglo-American Society* (1979), deserve special mention. A selection of extracts from the sources is in D. B. Quinn, *New American World*, vol. 5 (1978). It is now easy for readers to make their own judgment on John Smith with the help of P. L. Barbour, ed., *The Complete Works of Captain John Smith*, 3 vols. (1986).

On colonial cities, V. Fraser, *The Architecture of Conquest: Building in the Viceroyalty of Peru, 1535–1635* (1990), is important and also reveals much that is surprising about the roles of religious orders and native labor in monumental building. The exhibition catalogue *Ciudades hispanoamericanas* (1992) is invaluable for visual material, as is S. Lombardo de Ruiz et al., eds., *Atlás histórico de la ciudad de México*, vol. 1 (1996).

The remarkable little book by J. H. Elliott, *The Old World and the New* (1970), must be the starting point for any work on the mutual influence of Europe and the Americas in the colonial period. On ideas of savagery and related topics, important contributions include A. R. Pagden, *European Encounters with the New World: From Renaissance to Romanticism* (1993) and *The Fall of Natural Man: The American Indian and the Origins of Comparative Ethnology* (1982); B. C. Trigger, *Natives and Newcomers: Canada's Heroic*

Age Reconsidered (1985); M. Hodgen, *Early Anthropology in the Sixteenth and Seventeenth Centuries* (1962); S. Greenblatt, ed., *New World Encounters* (1993); and P. Hulme, *Colonial Encounters: Europe and the Native Caribbean* (1987).

On silver production and its impact, the best account is in V. Magalhães Godinho, *Os descubrimentos e a economia mundial,* 4 vols. (1983–1985); see also H. E. Cross, "South American Bullion Production and Export, 1550–1750," in J. F. Richards, ed., *Precious Metals in the Later Medieval and Early Modern Worlds* (1983); A. Attman, *American Bullion in the European World Trade, 1600–1800* (1986); W. Barrett, "World Bullion Flows, 1450–1800," in J. D. Tracy, ed., *The Rise of Merchant Empires: Long-distance Trade in the Early Modern World, 1350–1750* (1991). C. R. Phillips, "Trade in the Iberian Empires," ibid., is an invaluable summary that puts the issue of trade in perspective. Wider perspectives still are provided by P. D. Curtin, *Cross-Cultural Trade in World History* (1984), and I. Wallerstein, *The Modern World System,* vol. 1 (1970). A. Gunder Frank, *ReOrient: Global Economy in the Asian Age* (1998), and K. Pomeranz, *The Great Divergence: China, Europe and the Making of the Modern World Economy* (2000), take a commendably large view, looking at the distribution of resources in general. For the context in world history in very long-term perspective, see F. Fernández-Armesto, *Millennium,* latest ed. (1999).

For the ecology of New World imperialism, the work of A. W. Crosby is indispensable: *The Columbian Exchange* (1972); *Ecological Imperialism* (1986); and *Germs, Seeds and Animals: Studies in Ecological History* (1994). See also C. Galloway, *New Worlds for All: Indians, Europeans and the Remaking of Early America* (1997); W. Cronon, *Changes in the Land: Indians, Colonists and the Ecology of New England* (1983); G. Melville, *A Plague of Sheep: Environmental Consequences of the Conquest of Mexico* (1994); and M. Williams, *Americans and Their Forests* (1995).

On the "Kingdom of Patagonia," see C. Morales Gorleri, *El rey de Patagonia: Orélie Antoine I, Rey de Araucania y Patagonia* (1999);

on Ochogavia, J. de Carvajal, *Descubrimiento del río Apure,* ed. J. Alcina (1985).

CHAPTER 4: THE INDEPENDENCE ERA

On the landward growth of Brazil, see C. R. Boxer, *The Golden Age of Brazil* (1962), and J. Hemming, *Red Gold: The Conquest of the Brazilian Indians* (1978), which is also the best comprehensive study of the treatment of the native peoples in any of the European colonies. On France's colonial problems, S. Marzagalli, "The French Atlantic," *Itinerario,* 23 (1999), no. 2, is the best introduction.

G. Kubler and M. Soria, *Art and Architecture in Spain and Portugal and Their American Dominions, 1500 to 1800* (1959), is a comprehensive guide. The growing ambition of northern artists and their patrons can be traced in F. Kimball, *Domestic Architecture of the American Colonies and the Early Republic* (1922), and R. Bushman, *The Refinement of America: Persons, Houses, Cities* (1992).

The characterization of early colonial government as "feudal" was proposed and developed by C. Verlinden, *Les origines de la civilisation atlantique* (1966).

On colonial identity formation and creolism, see C. Kidd, *British Identities Before Nationalism, 1600–1800* (1999); N. Canny and A. Pagden, eds., *Colonial Identity in the Atlantic World, 1500–1800* (1987); F. Anderson, *Crucible of War: The Seven Years' War and the Fate of Empire in British North America, 1754–66* (2000); D. Brading, *The First America: The Spanish Monarchy, Creole Patriots and the Liberal State* (1991); J. Lafaye, *Quetzalcoatl y Guadalupe* (1985); and J. Cañizares-Esguerra, *How to Write the History of the New World* (2001). On Monticello, see J. McLaughlin, *Jefferson and Monticello* (1986), and S. R. Stein, *The Worlds of Thomas Jefferson at Monticello* (1993).

For the other aspects I mention of the intellectual background to the revolutions, see J.G.A. Pocock, *The Machiavellian Moment* (1975); C. Robbins, *The Eighteenth-Century Commonwealthmen* (1959); B. Bailyn, *The Ideological Origins of the American Revolu-*

tion (1967); D. Armitage, *The Intellectual Origins of the American Revolution;* F. Venturi, *Utopia and Reform in the Enlightenment* (1971); R. A. Ferguson, *The American Enlightenment, 1750–1820* (1994); and A. R. Pagden, *Lords of All the World* (1995).

On the demographic background in British America, three works are fundamental: B. Bailyn, *The Peopling of British North America: An Introduction* (1986) and *Voyagers to the West: A Passage in the Peopling of North America on the Eve of the Revolution* (1986), and J. M. Sosin, *Revolutionary Frontier, 1763–83* (1967). The economic background is surveyed in S. L. Engerman and R. E. Gallman, eds., *The Cambridge Economic History of the United States,* vol. 1: *The Colonial Era* (1996), and J. J. McKusker and R. R. Menard, *The Economy of British America, 1607–1789* (1985). For New England in particular, see D. S. Lovejoy, *Rhode Island Politics and the American Revolution, 1760–76* (1909); B. W. Labaree, *The Boston Tea Party* (1964); J. R. Daniel, *Experiment in Republicanism: New Hampshire Politics and the American Revolution* (1970); R. D. Brown, *Revolutionary Politics in Massachusetts* (1970). For the economic history of New England's maritime turn, see C. Leigh Heyrman, *Commerce and Culture: The Maritime Communities of Colonial Massachusetts, 1690–1750* (1984), and D. Vickers, *Farmers and Fishermen: Two Centuries of Work in Essex County, Massachusetts* (1994).

The correspondences with Latin America become apparent when one turns to D. A. Brading, *Miners and Merchants in Bourbon Mexico, 1763–1810* (1971); J. L. Phelan, *The People and the King: The Comunero Revolution in Colombia* (1978); A. J. Kuethe, *Military Reform and Society in New Granada, 1773–1808* (1978); J. Lynch, *The Spanish American Revolutions, 1808–26* (1973); M. P. Costeloe, *Response to Revolution: Imperial Spain and the Spanish American Revolutions, 1810–40* (1986).

On Malaspina, see A.C.F. David et al., eds., *The Diario of Alejandro de Malaspina* (2002). For Burr I rely on M. Lomask, *Aaron Burr,* 2 vols. (1979).

Representative studies of caudillismo include D. E. Stevens, *Origins of Instability in Early Republican Mexico* (1991); J. Lynch, *Ar-*

gentine Dictator: Juan Manuel de Rosas, 1829–52 (1981); and F. M. Nunn, *The Military in Chilean History, 1810–1973* (1976).

CHAPTER 5: INDEPENDENCE: THE NEW DEPENDENCY

L. Bethell, ed., *The Cambridge History of Latin America,* vol. 3: *From Independence to c. 1870* (1985), and vols. 4 and 5: *c. 1870–1930* (1986) cover the ground for Latin America. J. M. Burnsted, ed., *Interpreting Canada's Past,* 2 vols. (1993), is the most stimulating general history of Canada known to me.

There is a new edition of A. de Tocqueville, *Democracy in America,* ed. H. C. Mansfield and D. Winthrop (2000). C. Williamson, *American Suffrage from Property to Democracy, 1760–1860* (1960), traces the growth of the franchise. Travelers' accounts of American democracy are anthologized in M. Pachter and F. Wiren, eds., *Abroad in America: Visitors to the New Nation* (1976).

On dependency, see the classic work by F. H. Cardos and E. Faletto, *Dependency and Development in Latin America* (1979); the provocative L. E. Harrison, *Underdevelopment Is a State of Mind: The Latin American Case* (1985); the brilliant critique of J. Dunkerley, *Americana: The Americas in the World, Around 1850 (or "Seeing the Elephant" as The theme for an Imaginary Western)* (2000); S. Lebergott, *The Americas: An Economic Record;* D.C.M. Platt, "Dependency in XIXth-Century Latin America," *Latin American Research Review,* 15 (1980); J. Cotsworth and A. Taylor, eds., *Latin America and the World Economy Since 1800* (1998); and V. Bulmer-Thomas, *The Economic History of Latin America Since Independence* (1994).

On U.S. industrialization, see D. C. North, *The Economic Growth of the United States* (1966). The domestication of the prairie is one of those glaringly important subjects that has never found a historian. While waiting, see W. Cronon, *Nature's Metropolis: Chicago and the Great West* (1991). The analogy with the pampa can be seen in R. Mandrini, "Las fronteras y la sociedad indígena en el ámbito pampeano," *Anuario del IHES,* 12 (1997), 216–226.

My allusions to Trollope and Nora Mackinnon respectively

come from A. Trollope, *North America*, vol. 1 (2001), and N. Mackinnon, *An Estancia in Patagonia* (1997).

On the frontier, the starting point for all study and controversy is F. J. Turner, *The Frontier in American History* (I have used the 1920 edition). On Foraker, see E. Walters, *Joseph Benson Foraker* (1948). H. E. Bolton introduced the concept of the multilinear frontier in his extensive and always brilliant oeuvre. The best way into the controversy is through J. H. Elliott's freestanding lecture, "Do the Americas Have a Common History?" (1998). D. Weber, *The Spanish Frontier in North America* (1992), surveys the frontier Bolton opened to study with up-to-date scholarship. A. Hennessy, *The Frontier in Latin American History* (1970), extends the concept to Latin America.

E. H. Spicer, *The American Indians* (1980), is a brief guide to the history of the native peoples of the United States. For the mental dimension, see R. H. Pearce, *Savagism and Civilization. The Indian and the American Mind* (1967). On the plains, see R. White, "The Winning of the West: The Expansion of the Western Sioux in the Eighteenth and Nineteenth Centuries," *Journal of American History,* 65 (1978), 319–343; R. B. Hassrick, *The Sioux: Life and Customs of a Warrior Society* (1964); and P. H. Carlson, *The Plains Indians* (1998). For Tierra del Fuego, I rely on M. Gusinde, *Los indios de Tierra del Fuego,* 3 vols. (1982), and A. Chapman, *Drama and Power in a Hunting Society: The Selk'nam of Tierra del Fuego* (1982).

On emancipation and its circumstances and aftermath, see J. McPherson, *Battle Cry of Freedom: The Civil War Era* (1995); R. W. Fogel, *Without Consent or Contract: The Rise and Fall of American Slavery* (1989); L. Perry and M. Fellman, *Antislavery Reconsidered: New Perspectives on the Abolitionists* (1979); E. D. Genovese, *The Political Economy of Slavery: Studies in the Economy and Society of the Slave South* (1989); R. Conrad, *The Destruction of Brazilian Slavery, 1850–88;* T. E. Skidmore, *Black into White: Race and Nationality in Brazilian Thought* (1974); R. J. Scott, *Slave Emancipation in Cuba: The Transition to Free Labor, 1860–99* (1986). My lines on emancipation in war conditions are based on B. J. Fields et al., eds., *Free-*

dom: A Documentary History of Emancipation, 1861–7, vol. 1: *The Destruction of Slavery* (1985).

For black religion in Brazil, I rely on R. Lody, *O Povo do Santo: Religião, história e cultura dos Orixas, Voduns, Iquices e Caboclos* (1995); S. Bramly, *Macumba: The Teachings of Maria-Jose, Mother of the Gods* (1975); D. J. Jess and R. A. Da Matta, eds., *The Brazilian Puzzle: Culture on the Badlands of the West* (1995); J. H. Rodrigues, *Brazil and Africa* (1965); and R. Ireland, *Kingdoms Come: Religion and Politics in Brazil* (1991). For the influence of black religion on whites see D. Hess, *Samba in the Night: Spiritualism in Brazil* (1994), and on U.S. black Islam, C. E. Lincoln, *The Black Muslims in America* (1973).

CHAPTER 6: THE AMERICAN CENTURY

T. E. Skidmore and P. H. Smith, *Modern Latin America* (1989), is an indispensable guide to the history of the region in the nineteenth and twentieth centuries, complemented by T. H. Donghi, *The Contemporary History of Latin America* (1993). There is no history of twentieth-century North America, but for the United States, H. Evans, *The American Century* (1992), cuts a dash through the material, and the period since 1929 to 1974 is handled with verve and authority by D. M. Kennedy, *Freedom from Fear* (1999), and J. Patterson, *Grand Expectations* (1998).

The starting point on U.S. imperialism must be J. A. Field, "American Imperialism: The Worst Chapter in Almost Any Book," *American Historical Review,* 83 (1978). Important case studies of interventions include D. G. Munro, *Intervention and Dollar Diplomacy in the Caribbean, 1900–21* (1964); R. Immerman, *The CIA in Guatemala: The Foreign Policy of Intervention* (1982); W. LaFeber, *Inevitable Revolutions: The United States and Central America* (1983); and the whistle-blowing P. Agee, *Inside the Company: CIA Diary* (1975). I rely on R. Carr, *Puerto Rico: A Colonial Experiment* (1984), and H. Thomas, *Cuba or the Pursuit of Freedom* (1971), for their respective subjects.

C. Rangel, *The Latin Americans: Their Love-Hate Relationship with the U.S.* (1977), offers an intriguing sideways look at U.S.–Latin American relations, which are treated systematically in A. F. Lowenthal, *Partners in Conflict: The U.S. and Latin America* (1987); important case studies include J. Zoraida Vazquez and L. Meyer, *The U.S. and Mexico* (1985); P. Davis, *Where Is Nicaragua?* (1987); and, on Cuba, W. Smith, *The Closest of Enemies* (1987), and R. F. Smith, *The U.S. and Cuba: The Making of a Revolution* (1970).

On business imperialism, see D.C.M. Platt, *Business Imperialism, 1840–1930* (1977); H. Blakemore, *British Nitrates and Chilean Politics, 1886–96: Balmaceda and North* (1974); D. M. Pletcher, *Rails, Mines and Progress: Seven American Promoters in Mexico, 1867–1911* (1958).

The story of Pollard is told in H.B.C. Pollard, *A Busy Time in Mexico* (1913). M. Wilkins, *The Emergence of Multinational Enterprise: American Business Abroad from the Colonial Era to 1914* (1970), supplies the broad background.

For understanding the Allende case, the most helpful work I have found is by A. Angell, *Politics and the Labour Movement in Chile* (1972); A. Valenzuela, *The Breakdown of Democratic Regimes: Chile* (1978); P. Winn, *Weavers of Revolution: The Yarur Workers and Chile's Road to Socialism* (1986).

My sketches of particular countries rely mainly on a few standard works. On Argentina: D. Rock, *Politics in Argentina, 1890–1930: The Rise and Fall of Radicalism* (1975); J. Scobie, *Buenos Aires: From Plaza to Suburb, 1870–1910* (1974); J. A. Page, *Perón: A Biography* (1983); and G. W. Wynia, *Argentina: Illusions and Realities* (1986). On Chile: S. Collier and W. F. Sater, *A History of Chile* (1996); L. Gross, *The Last Best Hope: Eduardo Frei and Chilean Democracy* (1967); A. Valenzuela et al., eds., *Military Rule in Chile: Dictatorship and Oppositions* (1986); and P. Neruda, *Memoirs* (1977), have many instructive sidelights. On Uruguay: C. G. Gillespie, *Negotiating Democracy: Politicians and Generals in Uruguay* (1991), and M. G. Gilio, *The Tupamaros* (1972), which is partisan but useful. On Mexico: M. C. Meyer and W. L. Sherman, *The Course of Mexican History* (1987); A. Knight, *The Mexican Revolution*, 2 vols.

(1986)—a work of monumental scholarship with startling insights or stories on every page; J. Womack, *Zapata and the Mexican Revolution* (1958). On Brazil: T. E. Skidmore, *Brazil: Five Centuries of Change* (1999), is a model of *multum in parvo*—comprehensive and unerringly judicious.

Hispanic migration into the United States can be approached through R. O. de la Garza et al., eds., *The Mexican-American Experience: An Interdisciplinary Anthology* (1985); E. Acosta-Belen and B. Sjorstrom, eds., *The Hispanic Experience in the U.S.* (1988); and J. Gomoez-Quinones, *Chicano Politics: Reality and Promise* (1990).

My sketch of the beginnings of U.S. worldwide influence draws material from T. Hall, *The Spiritualists* (1962); J. E. Hasse, ed., *Ragtime: Its History, Composers and Music* (1985); M. Kimmelman, "A Century of Art: Just How American Was It?," *The New York Times,* April 18, 1999; and R. Hughes, *The Shock of the New* (1991). See G. Wilson Allen, *William James: A Biography* (1967). For Franz Boas, G. Stocking, ed., *The Shaping of American Anthropology, 1883–1911: A Franz Boas Reader* (1974), is the perfect introduction.

On the Americanist heresy, I have used M. J. Kirk, *The Spirituality of Thomas Hecker: Reconciling the American Character and the Catholic Faith* (1988), and J. Farina, ed., *Hecker Studies: Essays on the Thought of Isaac Hecker* (1983).

CHAPTER 7: RETROSPECT AND PROSPECTS: GRINGOS AND GO-GETTERS

T. J. Archdeacon, *Becoming American: An Ethnic History* (1983), and T. Coleman, *Passage to America* (1972), set Know-Nothingism and anti-Catholicism in the context of the growth through immigration of the Catholic community in the United States. See also J. Hannessy, *American Catholics: A History of the Roman Catholic Community in the United States* (1981); J. Dolan, *The American Catholic Experience: A Social History from Colonial Times to the Present* (1985); P. Gleason, *Keeping Faith: American Catholicism Past and Present* (1987); and R. Billington, *The Protestant Crusade, 1800–60* (1938).

On Latin Protestantism, the main authority is D. Martin, *Tongues of Fire: The Explosion of Protestantism in Latin America* (1990).

My remark about membership was inspired by N. L. Rosenblum, *Membership and Morals* (1998).

On the failure of socialism in America, S. M. Lipset and G. Marks, *It Didn't Happen Here: Why Socialism Failed in the U.S.* (2000), is the most searching work.

The apostle of climatic determinism and of the inherent superiority of North America (and, more specifically, of New England) was E. Huntington; see his *Civilization and Climate* (1922).

The final admonitions are those of J. Enríquez Cabot, *El reto de México: Tecnología y fronteras en el siglo*, vol. 21 (2000).

INDEX

Adams, John Quincy, 124–25
Africa:
    slave trade in, 59, 63, 64–66,
        93, 146
    as source of culture, 65,
        157–58
agriculture:
    early, 27–33, 42, 45, 51, 52
    industrialization of, 138–41
Aguirre, Lope de, 75
Ah Cacau, Mayan king, 36–37
Alarcón, Hernando de, 42
Aleijadinho, 110
Allende, Salvador, 168
alphabets, 41
Amazon River Valley, 50–51, 53,
    104
America:
    discovery of, 6–11, 77
    elasticity of term, 14–15
    name of, 5
"American dream," 176
American Revolution, 106,
        107–8, 112–13, 131–34
    and independence, 119–20,
        121, 126, 131

interventionism and,
        115–17
    success of, 117, 131
Americas:
    influence on world economy
        of, 81–83, 89–96
    influence on world history of,
        76–83
    as laboratory, 78–81
    maps, xi, xii, xiii, xiv
    multiplication of, 11–15
    natural resources in, 59–60,
        81, 85
    peopling of, 23–26
    unity of, 6–11
    see also Western Hemisphere
Andes:
    centers of civilization in,
        28–29, 40–41, 47, 52, 57,
        61–62
    environment of, 47–48, 201
    native populations in, 101
Anglo-Saxonism, 193–94
anthropology, 179
Antichrist, 75
Antipodes, 8–9

archaeology:
  on food production, 30
  on populations, 24–26
  on settlements, 44–45
architecture, 178
Argentina, 83, 165, 205
  development gap in, 181–84,
    187
  grasslands of, 140, 149, 182
  immigration to, 149
  independence of, 124
  literature of, 180
  natives exterminated in,
    84–85, 86, 152
Aristotle, 134–35
arts, 83, 108–11, 119
  Latin American influence on,
    179–80
  U.S. influence on, 173–74,
    177–79
astronomy, 37
Aztecs, 30, 40, 44, 57–58, 62, 108,
    114, 119

ball games, 33, 39, 44, 45
Barlow, Joel, 120
Bastide, Roger, 73
beans, 31, 45
Benedict of Palermo, 71
black history, 154–58
Boas, Franz, 79
Bolívar, Simón, 75, 124
Bolivia, 168
Bolton, H. E., 148
Borja, Carlos, 77
Boston Tea Party, 108
Brazil, 12, 132, 199
  the arts in, 109–10
  black religion in, 70–73,
    157–58
  development gap in, 186–87
  frontier of, 140, 146, 149
  immigration to, 149

  independence of, 122, 123,
    126–27
  interior of, 104–5, 109
  natives massacred in, 88–89
  racial diversity in, 89, 156,
    157–58
  slavery in, 88, 146, 156
  trade with, 143, 165
  U.S. intervention in, 168
Brody, Hugh, 13–14
Brown, John, 111
Bryce, James, 174–75
Buffon, George-Louis, 10
Burr, Aaron, 124–26

Cabet, Étienne, 13, 197
Cabeza de Vaca, Alvar Núñez,
    114
Cabot, Juan Enríquez, 202
Cabral, Pedro Alvares, 109, 187
cacao, 36–37, 91
Cacapol, 151
Cahokia, 46
California:
  gold rush in, 90
  missions in, 92, 97
  statehood for, 131
  trade route of, 94
Canada, 12, 132, 199, 200
  British investment in, 144–45
  development model of, 203–4
  English colony in, 112,
    121–22, 131
  and exceptionalism, 15, 16,
    18–19
  French colony in, 66, 121–22
  frontier of, 146–50
  natural resources in, 60, 139
Cangapol "el Bravo," 151
cannibalism, 80
Caribbean:
  emancipation in, 156
  English colonies in, 64, 97

Spanish colonies in, 58, 112
sugar grown in, 59, 104
Carolinas:
    maroon state in, 66
    population of, 106
    rice in, 59, 104
Carter, Jimmy, 95
Carver, George Washington, 95
Casas Grandes, Sinaloa, 44–45
Castilian language, 97
Castro, Fidel, 167–68
caudillismo, 124, 127, 136
Central America:
    early people of, 30, 47
    united republic of, 124
    see also Latin America;
        Mesoamerica
Chaco Canyon, 45, 49
Chan Chan, 48–49
Chávez, Hugo, 169
Chavín de Huantar, 29
Cherokee, 41
Chichimeca peoples, 44
Chile, 92, 195, 201
    Araucania in, 85, 149, 151
    development gap in, 184, 187
    natives exterminated in, 84,
        85–86
    natural resources in, 85, 140
    U.S. intervention in, 168
chili, 95
China trade, 81, 95, 109, 143
Choque Casa, Don Cristóbal,
    68–69
Christianity, 67–76
cities:
    in colonial world, 60–61, 97
    in early civilizations, 42–44, 52
    and industrialization, 138
    on trade routes, 91–92
citizenship, 111
civilization:
    the arts, 83, 108–11

centers of, 33–42
in cities, 42–44, 52, 60–61, 97
climatic theory of, 201–2
diffusionist theory of, 34
distribution of, 52–53
earliest, 26–33
European influence on, 57–69
food production in, 27–33, 42,
    45, 51, 52
Mayan, 35–40
Olmec, 33–35
transmission of, 42–47
writing systems of, 37, 39–42,
    80
civil liberties, basis of, 66–67
Clay, Henry, 135
climatic theory, 201–2
Clovis people, 24
coevolution, 28
Colombia:
    conquest of, 103
    democracy in, 198–99
    drug trade of, 164
colonies:
    acts of resistance by, 107–8
    countercolonialism, 169–73
    creole mentality in, 118–20
    dependency of, 141–46
    European influence on, 57–69,
        77, 96, 112–13, 115–17
    immigration into, 101–2
    landward drift of, 101–8
    map, xii
    maritime empires, 59, 94, 103,
        106–8, 142–44
    militarization of, 116–17, 121
    pioneering enterprise in, 114
    political rule of, 96–97
    religions in, 66–76
    of Spain, *see* Spanish colonies
    sustainable birthrates in, 101
    trade and commerce in, 90–93
    wealth creation in, 143–44

colonies (cont'd)
Western Hemisphere bonded
by, 83–96
in world history, 76–83
Columbian exchange, 78, 173
Columbus, Christopher, 6, 7–9,
57, 60, 62, 74, 77, 79, 82,
103
communism, 166–69, 188, 195
Condamine, Charles Marie de la,
78, 83
constitutions, written, 111, 112,
123, 127, 174
Cooper, James Fenimore, 139
Copán, Honduras, 38
Coronado, Francisco de, 90
Cortés, Hernando, 43, 62, 74, 77,
114
Cotton, John, 76
Counter-Reformation, 70, 71, 72
creole mentality, 118–20
Crèvecoeur, Michel-Guillaume
de, 106, 119–20
Crosby, Alfred, 78
Cuba, 149, 156, 163, 164
and communism, 167–68, 188,
195
railway system of, 201
cultural theories, 79, 200–201
Cunha, Manuel da, 110

Dana, Richard Henry, 94
Darío, Rubén, 180
Darwin, Charles, 78, 153–54
David, Jacques-Louis, 111
Debussy, Claude, 177
Declaration of Independence,
U.S., 118, 127, 175–76
de la Cruz, Fray Francisco, 75
de la Cruz, Sor Juana, 108
democracy:
achievements of, 136, 200
and anti-imperialism, 170

free association of citizens in,
111, 134, 135, 196–97
and independence, 111,
134–37
model of, 133, 174–75, 176,
188, 199, 203–4
shortcomings of, 135
town councils in, 114–15
democratization, 133–36, 200
De Pauw, Cornelius, 10
deserts, 48–49
de Soto, Hernando, 42
Díaz, Porfirio, 185, 199–200
diffusionist theory, 34
Dominican Republic, 168, 171
Dulles, John Foster, 166–67
Dutch colonies, 63, 109, 163
Dvorák, Antonin, 177

earthworks, 28, 32–33, 45–46
Edwards, Jonathan, 73
Elesbaan, Saint, 71
England:
and the arts, 108–9, 111
colonial quarrels with, 107–8
colonies of, 58, 60, 62–64, 97,
101, 105–6, 111, 112, 115,
121–22, 131, 132, 142
Indians exterminated by, 86–88
interventionism of, 115–17
investments in New World,
144–45, 165–66
trade with, 115
Enlightenment, 80–81
environmental matrix, 47–52
climatic theories, 201–2
conquest of, 139–40
deserts, 48–49
diversity in, 49–50
equator, 50
frontiers of, 152–54
insufficiencies of, 49–50
lowlands, 50–51

mountains, 47–48
temperate zone, 50–52
underexploited, 206
Eratosthenes, 8
Esmeraldas, 65–66, 90
Etzler, John Adolphus, 13
Europe:
    American influence on, 76–83,
        89–96, 173–80
    colonies of, 57–69
    development gap in, 192–94
    diseases from, 50–51, 61, 143,
        154
    industrialization in, 137
    influence of, 57–69, 77, 96,
        112–13, 115–17
    investments in New World,
        144–45
    livestock from, 150–51, 153
    religion in, 69–70
    revolutions in, 112–13
    and world economy, 81–83,
        145–46
    World Wars in, 166, 170
evolution, 78, 153–54
exceptionalism, 15–19
extinctions, 25
extirpators, 69

Florida, 66, 87, 97
Fourier, Charles, 13, 197
France:
    colonies of, 16, 58, 60, 62, 66,
        101, 102, 105, 121–22
    missionaries from, 66
French Revolution, 121, 135, 173,
    175
Frobisher, Martin, 60
frontier, 146–50, 163
Fuentes, Carlos, 172

Galápagos, 78
Galves, Alonso Sánchez, 65–66

Gálvez, Manuel, 182
García Márquez, Gabriel, 180
Gaspée, seizure of, 108
Georgia, 64, 95, 106
glyphs, 40
Golden Number, 61
gold mining, 90, 103, 154
Goulart, João, 168
gourds, 31
Graffigny, Françoise de, 41
Grant, Ulysses S., 136
Great Awakening, 73
Great Lakes, 46–47
Grenada, 164, 168
Guatemala, 167, 195
Guzmán, Abimael, 75

Haiti, 112, 121, 163
Hamilton, Alexander, 125
Haya, Victor Raúl, 75
Helsinki Process, 176
Hennessy, Alistair, 146
Hispaniola, 57, 103, 104
horses, 150–51
Huarochirí, Peru, 68
Huiliches people, 97
humanists, 8, 112
human rights, 79, 111, 175–77
Humboldt, Alexander von, 78, 120
Humboldt Current, 92
Hunahpu, 38–39
Huntington, Samuel, 202
Hurons, 80–81, 91

immigration, 101–2, 106, 137–38,
    149, 172
import substitution, 143
Inca world, 29–30, 41, 57–58, 75
independence:
    American Revolution, 119–20,
        121, 126, 131
    and business imperialism,
        144–46

independence (cont'd)
    democracy and, 111, 134–37
    emergence of, 121–27
    immigration and, 137–38
    industrialization and, 137, 138, 141
    landward movement and, 101–8, 115
    moving toward, 107–8, 111–21
    U.S. strength in, 117, 131–34, 138–40
India, trade with, 81, 95, 109, 143
industrialization, 133, 136–41, 202, 205
Iphigenia, Saint, 71–72
Ireland, 14
Iroquois, 32, 47, 62, 80
Isthmus of Panama, 92, 163
Ixbalanqué, 38–39
Ixtlilxochitl, Fernando de Alva, 118

Jackson, Andrew, 135
Jamaica, 66, 97, 156, 171
James, William, 179
jazz, 177
Jefferson, Thomas, 10, 116, 119–20, 125
Jerusalem artichoke, 31

Kennedy, John F., 168
King Philip's War, 87–88

Lahontan, Louis-Armand de, 80
Las Casas, Bartolomé de, 78–79
Latin America, 16
    black history in, 157–58
    cheap labor in, 137
    colonies in, see colonies
    communism and, 166–69
    democracy in, 133
    dependency in, 142–46
    economies of, 201, 202, 205
    frontier in, 146–50
    independence in, 123–24, 175
    influence of, 172–73, 179–80
    monocultures in, 136–37, 202–3
    native peoples in, 150–54
    trade with, 164–66
    underdevelopment of, 137, 202–6
    U.S. interference in, 164, 168–69
Latino music and culture, 180
laws, codified, 111, 114–15, 127
Lima, Peru, 61
Lincoln, Abraham, 157
Louisiana, 93–94, 105, 131
Lynch, Eliza, 111

Machiavelli, Niccolò, 112
Mackenzie, Alexander, 131
Mackinnon, Nora, 141
maize, 30–32, 44, 45, 51, 94
Malaspina, Alejandro, 120–21
Mandan people, 97
manioc, 51
Mansfield, Lord, 155
maps:
    Americas, xiv
    Americas (1830), xiii
    Colonials (c. 1650), xii
    Diversity of Central and South America, xi
    pictograms as, 42
Mapuche, 84, 85–86
Marajó mounds, 51
María José, 73
maroon kingdoms, 65–66
Marx, Karl, 197
Maryland, Catholicism in, 67, 193, 194
Mayan culture, 35–40, 42, 119, 150

Mesoamerica:
    ball game in, 33, 39, 45
    centers of civilization in,
        30–31, 33–35, 42–46, 52,
        57, 61–62, 201
    native populations in, 101
    transmission of culture from,
        42–47
Mexican Revolution, 164, 169,
    199
Mexican War, 131, 166
Mexico, 12–13, 16, 43
    ball game in, 33
    conquest of, 103, 114
    creole mentality in, 119
    development gap in, 185–86
    early civilization in, 47, 52
    food production in, 30
    frontier of, 149–50
    and the future, 202–3
    independence of, 122, 124
    influence of, 82, 92, 172
    instability in, 199–200
    loss of territory by, 131, 150,
        166, 194
    nomad wars in, 44
    printing presses in, 108
    religion in, 68, 74, 195
    stranger effect in, 113
    trade routes of, 91, 92
    U.S. investment in, 164
Mexico City, 61, 186
migrations, 23–25, 102
Minas Gerais, 90, 110
mining, 89, 90, 92
miscegenation, 133
missionaries, 60, 66, 67–68, 71,
    73, 74–75, 79–80, 92, 97,
    154, 172
Mississippi River, 46, 93–94
Mixtec histories, 40
Moche civilization, 48–49
Monroe Doctrine, 10, 165

Montaigne, 80
Monticello, 119–20
mound builders, 28, 45–46, 51
mountains, 47–48
munitions industry, 95

NAFTA (North American Free
    Trade Association), 16
Napoleonic Wars, 122, 131
Native Americans:
    arts of, 110
    as cheap labor, 144
    common threads among,
        35–36
    control of, 62–63
    diseases brought to, 50–51, 61,
        143, 154
    enforced integration of, 149
    eradication of, 84–89, 149,
        150–54
    food production by, 30–32
    human status of, 79
    and missionaries, 60, 66, 67–68,
        71, 73, 79–80, 97, 154
    as noble savages, 79–81
    origin myths of, 13–14, 23, 44
    political interaction with, 114
    populations of, 101, 133
    religions of, 69–70, 72, 74
    as slaves, 88–89
    and the stranger effect, 113
natural resources, 59–60, 78, 81,
    85, 93, 139–40
Nazca, 49
Neruda, Pablo, 180
New England:
    King Philip's War in, 87–88
    marine economy of, 59, 94,
        103, 106–8
    migration from, 102
    population in, 102
    religion in, 67, 193
    revolution in, 112–13

New Mexico, 66, 87, 103–4, 148
New World, 5, 9–10
    indigenous peoples of, 14
    investment in, 144–45, 165–66
    noble savages in, 79
    religion in, 74–75
    trade with, 143–46
    see also Western Hemisphere
Nicaragua, 164, 168, 195
Nigual (mapmaker), 42
Nixon, Richard M., 167
North America, 15–16
    big game in, 48, 89, 139, 140,
        152–53
    colonies in, 63–64; see also
        colonies
    food production in, 31, 94–96,
        138–41
    inland development of, 102–8
    native populations in, 41–42,
        86, 101, 151–52
    natural resources in, 60, 93
    as underdeveloped, 44, 49–50,
        51–52, 101, 204
    wealth gap in, 64, 137
Nuestra Señora de Guadalupe, 68

Oberá the Resplendent, 75
Ocelotl, Don Martín, 75
Ochogavia, Miguel de, 93
Ohio-Michigan War, 132
Old World, see Europe
Olmec culture, 33–35, 39–40
Organization of American States
    (OAS), 166
Ortega y Gasset, José, 182, 183
Owen, Robert, 197

Paine, Thomas, 112
Palenque ruins, 119
Palmares, kingdom of, 66
Panama, 92, 163, 164
Pan-American approach, 19

Pangea, 78
papaya, 51
Paraguay, 103, 124, 156
Patagonia, 140–41, 149, 150,
    152–53
Paul III, Pope, 79
peanuts, 95
Pearson, Weetman, 165
Pennsylvania, Quakers in, 67,
    86–87, 193, 194
Pernéty, Antoine-Joseph, 10
Perón, Juan, 182–83
Peru:
    conquest of, 92, 103
    creole mentality in, 119
    desert in, 48
    economy of, 82, 203
    independence of, 122
    maize produced in, 31
    printing presses in, 108
    trade routes of, 92
    Tres Ventanas cave, 27
Pharisaic theory of history,
    192–202
Philippines, 14–15, 143, 163,
    171
picture writing, 40, 42
plantations, 82, 89, 156
Pocahontas, 63
Pollard, Hugh, 165–66
Pope, Gen. John, 151
Popper, Julio, 154
Portugal:
    colonies of, 57–59, 63, 101,
        102, 104–5, 109, 113, 142,
        143
    and slave trade, 59, 63, 146
Posada, José, 166
potatoes, 31, 96
Potosí, 90
Puccini, Giacomo, 177
Puerto Rico, 16, 156, 163, 171
Puritans, 67, 193

Quakers, 67, 86–87, 193, 194
quipus, 41

ragtime, 177
Raleigh, Sir Walter, 90
Ramón, García, 84
ranching, 89–90
Reformation, 70, 191
religion, 66–76
    Age of the Holy Spirit, 75
    Anabaptism, 76
    Antichrist, 75
    black, 70–73, 157–58
    Catholicism, 66–70, 72–73,
        79, 172, 193–95
    charismatic, 73–74
    chiliastic, 75
    Christianity, 67–76, 96
    evangelization in, 74, 195
    Great Awakening, 73
    messianic, 75–76
    millenarianism, 74–76
    missionaries, 60, 66, 67–68,
        71, 73, 74–75, 79–80, 92,
        97, 154, 172
    pagan survivals, 68, 69–70, 72,
        157–58
    Protestantism, 67, 70, 76, 172,
        193–95
    spiritual conquest, 67–68
    Spiritualism, 75
    syncretic features, 68, 69
Renaissance, 8, 112
republicanism, 83, 111, 112
Requena, Francisco de, 51
Rhode Island, 67, 193
rice, 59, 104
rights of man, 79, 111, 175–77
Rios Montt, Efraín, 195
Roca, Gen. Julio Argentino, 84,
    152
Rodrigues, Nina, 73
Rolfe, John, 63

Romanticism, 82–83, 173
Rousseau, Jean-Jacques, 80, 112

Sagard, Father, 41
Salvador, 70–71
Sandinistas, 168, 195
Sandino, Augusto Cesar, 75
Sangro, Raimondo di, 41
San Lorenzo, 34
Sansevero, 41
Sarmiento, Domingo Faustino,
    152
science and technology, 179
scientific revolution, 77–78
Sendero Luminoso, 75
Seven Years' War, 117
Sioux, 42, 151–52
skyscrapers, 178
slaves:
    as cheap labor, 63, 64, 137, 144
    emancipation of, 154–57
    and human rights, 176
    native peoples as, 88–89
    numbers of, 114, 133, 156
    plantations, 89, 156
    and religion, 72–73
slave trade, 59, 63, 64–66, 93, 146
Smith, Adam, 77
Smith, John, 62–63, 113
socialism, 83, 167–68, 197
Sousa, John Philip, 177
South America:
    early civilizations in, 26–33
    early maps of, 6
    and equator, 50
    land empire in, 104
    see also Latin America
Spain:
    and the arts, 108–9, 111
    Catholicism of, 66–70
    colonies of, *see* Spanish
        colonies
    influence of, 62–64, 96–97

Spain (*cont'd*)
  interventionism of, 116–17
  trade and commerce with,
    91–93
Spanish colonies:
  cities of, 60–61, 97
  creole mentality in, 118–20
  cultural exchange in, 96–97,
    112
  early civilizations, 57–59
  economies of, 58–59, 62, 96
  fighting among, 132
  independence wars, 121, 122,
    123–24
  instability in, 197–98
  landward movement in, 101,
    102, 103–4
  of maroons, 65–66
  militarization of, 116–17, 121
  as model, 63, 64, 66, 105, 115
  modern state in, 112, 114–15
  and native cultures, 58–59, 61
  plantations in, 156
  religion in, 67–70, 74–76, 96,
    97
  and slave trade, 59, 63, 93
  stagnation of, 111, 131,
    132–34
  stranger effect in, 113–14
  trade among, 143
spiritualism, 174
Spiro, Oklahoma, 46
squash, 31, 45
Strabo, 8
sugar, 59, 104
Sullivan, Louis, 178
Surinam, 66
sweet potatoes, 31

Tapajó people, 51
Taylor, Zachary, 136
technology, 179, 202–3, 205–6
Tehuacán, 31

Teixeira, Pedro, 92–93
Teotihuacán, 30, 43, 46
Texas, 131
Thoreau, Henry David, 170
Tiahuanaco, 29–30
Tierra del Fuego, 78, 152–53
timekeeping, priestly, 37–38, 119
tobacco, 59, 63, 104
Tocqueville, Alexis de, 134–35,
    136, 174
tomatoes, 95–96
totalitarianism, 162
trade and commerce, 89, 90–93
  biota transfers in, 94–96
  business imperialism, 162–69
  globalization of, 205–6
  independence and, 123,
    142–46
  sea vs. land, 103
  in slaves, 59, 63, 64–66, 93,
    146
  wealth via, 115
Tres Ventanas cave, Peru, 27
Trollope, Anthony, 139, 206
Tula "Garden of the Gods," 43
Turner, Frederick Jackson, 147,
    163
turquoise, 45
Twain, Mark, 170

Ugarte, Manuel, 163
United Fruit Company, 167
United States:
  agriculture in, 138–40
  business imperialism of,
    162–69
  civil war in, 123, 132, 138, 145,
    174
  communities in, 196–97
  constitution of, 123, 127
  countercolonization of,
    169–73
  democratization of, 133–36

entity of, 12, 200–201
exceptionalism of, 15–19
expansion of, 132
frontier in, 146–50, 163
hyphenated identities in,
    11–12, 172–73, 194
immigration to, 137–38, 149,
    172
imperial republic of, 162–69
industrialization of, 133,
    136–41, 202
influence of, 161–69, 173–88
internal rivalries in, 123
Latinization of, 172–73
Ohio-Michigan War, 132
peace within, 132
popular culture of, 177–79
population of, 200–201
strength of, 117, 126, 131–34,
    138–40, 161–62
Uruguay:
    democracy in, 198–99
    development gap in, 184–85
    grasslands of, 140
    immigration to, 149
    independence of, 124
Utopia, 135, 197

Valverde, Francisco, 42
Vancouver, George, 131
Vargas Llosa, Mario, 180
Vega, Garcilaso de la, 118
Venezuela, 124, 169, 198
Vermont, 155
Vespucci, Amerigo, 6
Vieira, António da, 72
Villagrá, Gaspar Pérez de, 44
Virginia:
    colonists of, 62–65, 101–2
    population of, 106
    slaves in, 65
    tobacco in, 59, 63, 104
    wealth gap in, 64

Virgin Islands, 163, 170, 171
Voltaire, 80–81

wage labor, 89, 90
Waldseemüller, Martin, 6
Washington, George, 116, 136
West, Benjamin, 111
Western Hemisphere:
    black history in, 154–58
    development gap in, 181–88
    disunity of, 11–15
    exceptionalism of, 15–19
    fabric of dependency in,
        141–46
    frontier in, 146–50
    indigenous peoples in, 150–54
    influence of, 76–83
    interior developed in, 101–8
    parallel histories in, 141
    revolutions in, 115–17,
        121–22, 131–34
    trade routes within, 91–93
    uniform capitalism in, 90
    unity of, 6–7, 9–10, 83–96
    wealth gap in, 137
wheat, 104
Wilson, Woodrow, 163, 170
World Wars, 166, 169–70
Wounded Knee, 88
Wright, Frank Lloyd, 178
writing systems, 37, 39–42, 80

Ximénez, Francisco, 38
Xochicalco, 119

Yaqui people, 150
Young, Brigham, 13
Yucatán, 66, 91

Zacatecas, 90
Zapata, Emilio, 76, 195
Zapotec people, 40
Zumbi, King, 66

About the Author

Felipe Fernández-Armesto is a professor in the departments of history and geography at Queen Mary, University of London, and a member of the Faculty of Modern History of Oxford University. His books, which have been translated into twenty-two languages, include *Columbus; Millennium; Civilizations: Culture, Ambition and the Transformations of Nature;* and *Near a Thousand Tables: A History of Food.*

A Note on the Type

The principal text of this Modern Library edition
was set in a digitized version of Janson, a typeface that
dates from about 1690 and was cut by Nicholas Kis,
a Hungarian working in Amsterdam. The original matrices have
survived and are held by the Stempel foundry in Germany.
Hermann Zapf redesigned some of the weights and sizes for
Stempel, basing his revisions on the original design.